W9-CFG-576

Effective Sales Force Automation and Customer Relationship Management

Effective Sales Force Automation and Customer Relationship Management

A Focus on Selection and Implementation

Raj Agnihotri
Adam A. Rapp

Effective Sales Force Automation and Customer Relationship Management
Copyright © Business Expert Press, LLC, 2010.

All rights reserved. No part of this publication may be reproduced, stored in a retrieval system, or transmitted in any form or by any means—electronic, mechanical, photocopy, recording, or any other except for brief quotations, not to exceed 400 words, without the prior permission of the publisher.

First published in 2010 by
Business Expert Press, LLC
222 East 46th Street, New York, NY 10017
www.businessexpertpress.com

ISBN-13: 978-1-60649-127-0 (paperback)
ISBN-10: 1-60649-127-X (paperback)

ISBN-13: 978-1-60649-128-7 (e-book)
ISBN-10: 1-60649-128-8 (e-book)

DOI 10.4128/9781606491287

A publication in the Business Expert Press Selling and Sales Force Management collection

Collection ISSN (print): Forthcoming
Collection ISSN (electronic): Forthcoming

Cover design by Jonathan Pennell
Interior design by Scribe Inc.

First edition: July 2010

10 9 8 7 6 5 4 3 2 1

Printed in the United States of America.

Abstract

As we move deeper into the 21st century, firms continue to struggle with the implementation of sales force technology tools and the role they play in sales representative performance. Foreseeing a changing environment, many sales organizations have begun to focus on technology-related strategies, business processes, and applications to adapt to these emerging issues.

With this in mind, sales force technology usage has changed the methods of selling. Salespeople are no longer selling just a "product"; instead, they are providing a valuable "solution" to customer problems. Salespeople now act as consultants or experts and provide customized solutions. This role requires salespeople to develop a technological orientation to access, analyze, and communicate information in order to establish a strong relationship with customers. Sales technology enables salespeople to answer the queries of customers and effectively provide competent solutions. The ability to answer queries and provide solutions leads to strong relationships between a salesperson and a customer. Thus, technology tools are not only used for smoothing the work process, but they also have strategic utilizations.

With the adoption of technological tools at exponential rates, many firms fell into pitfalls and witnessed failure of their technology initiatives. The purpose of this book is to outline the important steps that must be considered and adhered to when implementing sales force technology. Perhaps the most important aspect covered within this book is that technology usage is both a strategy and a tool; therefore, we outline both strategic considerations as well as implementation procedures throughout each chapter. It is important to consider all the steps and the necessary actions that will need to take place before the first penny is spent; then, and only then, will the technology have its intended effect.

Keywords

Sales teams, virtual, sales force management, leadership, selling centers, buying centers, sales technology, technology audit, relational selling, customer satisfaction, customer retention, customer loyalty

Contents

Introduction

This book describes the approaches and strategies related to sales force automation (SFA) and customer relationship management (CRM). Although corporations have embraced CRM as a key business strategy, many companies are still figuring out the best way to shape and execute this strategy. To address this problem, this book focuses on selection and implementation issues related to CRM.

In chapter 1, the use of sales technology is categorized into two dimensions, namely the use of SFA and the use of CRM, based on their level of specificity for influencing different salespersons' behaviors. To achieve the projected effects of technology, it is necessary to define different dimensions of technology usage and to outline both strategic considerations and implementation procedures for sales organizations.

In chapter 2, the discussion goes back to basics with an intention to find out what "marketing" means and why the focus in organizations is on a new form of marketing known as "relationship marketing." Later in the chapter, the question of how to devise an effective relationship strategy is addressed, and the enabling role of technology within this strategy is considered.

In chapter 3, customer-related outcomes take the center stage. Discussion involves different aspects of customer-company relationship such as customer satisfaction, customer retention, and customer loyalty. Technology innovations have made it easy for customers to get information and build networks. For firms it is essential to have strategies in place that enable them to operate in this new consumer-centric marketplace and to acquire, satisfy, and retain customers. Customer-oriented strategies related to each of these aspects will be critical for a firm's survival.

In chapter 4, attention is focused on decisions concerning CRM technology selection. Choosing a CRM software solution can easily become a hassle if not undertaken properly. Numerous CRM applications that differ from each other on multiple dimensions are available. An exhaustive scanning of the organization's internal environment and an assessment of needs, such as scope and functionality, are necessary before making a selection. Several other critical and related issues such as firm culture, its ability to adopt and learn, and the role of top management are also discussed in length.

Chapter 5 focuses on CRM planning, system design, and construction. Infrastructure is required for this, and the reengineering of current structures, systems, and processes are discussed in detail in this chapter.

In chapter 6, the attention is turned toward implementation. Related issues such as training programs, garnering support within the organization, and cascade of adoption are also discussed. In addition, the framework regarding CRM performance measurement is presented along with business and technological objectives. This chapter highlights the fact that because of its tactical and methodical nature, implementation of CRM does not happen overnight. Top management should execute this implementation process in steps, which are described in the chapter.

In chapter 7, the need for full integration is highlighted. The CRM integration process begins with the development of CRM culture, followed by the integration of technology applications into the value chain. The full integration of a CRM system into an organization's existing business architecture will require the establishment of CRM culture within the organization through company-wide awareness. The importance of full integration and approaches toward integration across channels are described in this chapter. Additionally, the chapter details the concept of customer lifetime value and the role of data analytics.

Chapter 8 covers the assessment of CRM technology and its maintenance. Technology audit, as a method of assessment, is described. This is a technique that aims to investigate technology capability, processes, and requirements of the concerned firm. The chapter concludes with a description of 10 basic steps that can be employed in conducting an organization's technology audit.

In order to provide readers with a better understanding of the contents, a case study is presented at the end of each chapter.

CHAPTER 1

Defining Technology

With the customer being the focal point and customer relationships being the central theme of many business strategies, organizations have witnessed countless opportunities created through technology advancements. These opportunities are especially prevalent in sales organizations, considering that they are responsible for creating links between firms and customers. Thus, many sales organizations have embraced technology to leverage the possibilities presented. Sales technology is a new mantra for sales organizations to gain success and build relationships. Firms are seeing the use of technology as a way of enhancing sales efficiency and sales effectiveness.

In today's era of market-oriented firms, where sales organizations have migrated from being a transactional-oriented entity to a relational-oriented entity, there are new labels for sales representatives, such as "relationship managers." In this transformed role, salespeople are responsible for achieving high customer-satisfaction levels. To achieve high levels of customer satisfaction, the sales representatives (hereafter, "sales reps") must learn about the customers and use that knowledge to design need-satisfying strategies. Additionally, for sales reps, technology use facilitates the process of knowledge attainment, which further improves their performance. In addition, through the use of relationship-building tasks, sales reps are exploring multiple dimensions of technology utilization (i.e., accessing, analyzing, and communicating information), which, in turn, are affecting different aspects of sales performance. Also, salespeople's technology orientation influences their internal role performance by smoothing the back-office tasks, enhancing communications, reducing cycle time, organizing information, and, consequently, enhancing efficiency.

Although sales technology has so much to offer, there is no scarcity of evidence outlining the history of *un*successful technology implementation

by sales organizations. In fact, more than half of sales technology investments are considered by top management to be unprofitable. One critical
reason for this conflicting evidence is that there is no clear formulation
of a technology concept for sales organizations. To achieve the projected
effects of technology, it is necessary to define different dimensions of
technology usage and outline both strategic considerations as well as
implementation procedures for sales organizations.

Sales Technology

Defined broadly, technology is "an ability to act, a competence to perform, translating materials, energy and information in one set of states
into another, more highly valued set of states."[1] For sales organizations,
sales technology is composed of tools and techniques that aid or enable
the sales task performance. Sales technology, in essence, is the adoption
and utilization of different technology tools to reengineer and automate
sales and marketing processes so that organizations improve their sales
and marketing effectiveness and, in turn, increase revenues. Successful
implementation of sales technology should support the selling process
from generating the lead to closing the deal.

In the past, issues concerning the different dimensions and aspects of
technology use have been raised. It is especially essential for a sales organization to address the diverse uses of technology and its differential effects
on salespeople's behavior. Individuals in an organization are supposed
to perform various tasks or activities to attain outputs, and technology
provides tools that help them to perform these tasks. The use of certain
applications of technology depends on the specific characteristics of the
assigned task. In any sales organization, sales reps perform operational
and administrative tasks (e.g., learning about new and existing product
lines, generating automated reports, communicating with other departments) as well as tactical and strategic tasks (e.g., identifying the most
important customers, preparing sales presentations based on customers'
specific needs and requirements). Depending on the nature of the task,
sales reps need particular tools to help perform these activities. The effect
of technology usage on sales reps' behavior will rely on the purpose of the
task and whether it is strategic or operational in nature.

Given the fact that different dimensions of technology usage should be employed for different purposes, management should create and support work settings where sales reps are encouraged to use technology in a proper fashion. Sales reps performing operational tasks (e.g., sharing information with colleagues and managers, monitoring inventory levels, or learning about products) should use different system applications when performing these tasks than when performing strategic tasks (e.g., identifying potential customers, identifying the most important customers from the list of potential customers, or working on improvement of sales presentation skills).

Understanding how different technology tools have diverse influence on performance-enhancing behaviors is advantageous for both management and sales reps. In light of that, we categorize the use of sales force automation (SFA) and the use of customer relationship management (CRM) as two dimensions of sales technology based on their level of specificity (e.g., automation of routine and administrative tasks or strategy-building tools) for influencing different salespersons' behaviors such as effort and adaptive selling. For example, SFA usage, with an operational orientation, comprises the utilization of technological tools supporting routine sales functions, while, as a strategic tool, CRM technology utilization includes devising methods and employing technology that help sales reps to develop sales strategies. For sales reps to build, maintain, and strengthen the relationships with customers, both routine sales tasks and strategic activities are equally important.

Sales technologies have evolved and developed quite dramatically over a short period of time. Similar to the change from an organization's orientation from product selling to solution selling, sales technology has witnessed some major transformations (Figure 1.1). In its early stages, technology was mainly used to support decisions focused on how to gain market share. Later, front-end applications such as sales analysis systems, sales integration systems, and the like emerged to address the changes in the marketplace. Currently, as companies seek to gain the share of the customer's mind, enterprise-wide CRM solutions are prevalent. Organizations that adopt enterprise value networks are striving for solution selling to provide customers with the highest possible value.

Organizations perceive sales technology as a means to improve sales force productivity and effectiveness because it helps them streamline

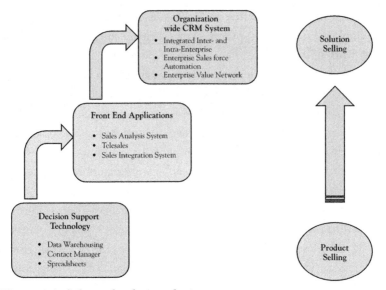

Figure 1.1. *Sales technology evolution.*

the flow of the business process (Figure 1.2). It also enables sales reps to know more information about more customers. Thus, sales technology is perceived as a contributor to customer satisfaction by improving communication, speeding responsiveness, and enhancing customer service. It

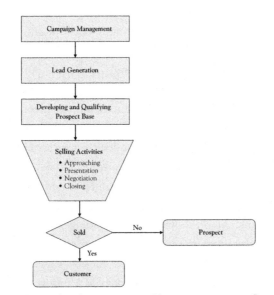

Figure 1.2. *Sales technology supported business process flow.*

increases effectiveness in management through supporting team selling, optimizing interactions, and reducing administration. With proper utilization of sales technology, sales cycles can be reduced and actual selling time can be increased, sales forecasts can be improved, costs can be decreased, and revenue can be increased.

Sales Force Automation

SFA is the application of technology to support regular sales functions and includes tools that are employed by users to perform administrative and other repetitive tasks. SFA transforms repetitive and routine manual processes to automated processes, which helps sales reps operate in a more efficient manner. For example, applications such as quarterly automated sales reports and calendaring tools are key elements of sales technology. The domain for SFA applications includes the attainment and storage of information. SFA tools assist sales reps in formulating a professional sales encounter. Sales reps can remain in contact with distant customers via e-mails and cell phones, thus reducing travel hours. They can also receive and manage orders from customers in an easy, timely fashion. Additionally, applications like calendaring and routing tables help sales reps reduce downtime and increase their own production during regular work hours.

To optimize the benefits of SFA, sales reps should be aware of the specific purposes of its use. With SFA, sales reps improve their productivity and competitiveness because the consistent and quick flow of information helps them to be more precise in their sales presentations. The assistance of SFA tools with routine tasks allows sales reps to focus more on relationship-building tasks rather than on administrative tasks. The use of SFA allows a sales force to optimize every step of its sales strategy, including presentations, informing, communications, and sales reporting. Sales reps in today's competitive environment are required to keep track of customers' priorities, competitor's activities, and product market situations. With special applications and other analytic database tools, SFA helps sales reps to manage market intelligence in a well-timed manner. Additionally, and as previously mentioned, salespeople will improve in terms of efficiency as the back-office operations, such as sales reporting, become automated.

Customer Relationship Management

In order to develop better relationships with customers, organizations want to understand the needs of customer and learn about their behaviors. CRM, when used as a strategic tool, has been utilized by organizations for these purposes. Use of CRM technology focuses on relationship and strategy building, is cross-functional in nature, and provides a platform for continuous interactions with customers. For organizations, CRM is a strategy for developing an integrated and comprehensive customer database with the help of information technology (IT). CRM databases deliver both relationship and analytic data that a firm needs to manage interactions, speed up workflows, anticipate opportunities, increase revenue, and reduce costs. Specifically, business analytic data can help find customers that are the most important based on the amount of products they buy and the cost of serving them. In addition, such data are helpful in managing the supply chain, as it can assess which suppliers deliver the quality products on time and at the most reasonable price.

One of the prominent players in the financial service industry, Wells Fargo, offers customers positive experiences with the help of a CRM technology called PeopleSoft Enterprise. Especially for its online services, Wells Fargo wanted to adopt and implement a customer-centric model. Wells Fargo's management was well aware that this vision could only be realized through a CRM solution that makes it possible for the company to serve *any customer at any time*. The company strategically implemented CRM technology and successfully achieved its goal of knowing its customers better. The CRM technology empowered them to offer value-oriented services and unique experiences throughout the customer life cycle. This approach can be replicated in other industries as well. For example, CRM systems can help companies running businesses within the airline industry, as they would be able to obtain business-class customer information of how often they fly and at what time of year, the purpose of the trip (i.e., business or personal), their food preferences, and so on. Access to such information will help the firm know what promotional material to send out, what new deals to promote to each customer, what preferences or options may be attractive to each customer, and when would be a good time to target each customer. The companies can use the information to build a relationship with the customer not only by reminding customers of flight cancellations or delays but also by sending birthday cards, for example.

Representing the analysis aspects of sales technology, CRM tools help sales reps develop and manage customer relationships. One can envision the functional use of CRM as a process that helps compile pieces of information about the customers, the firm's selling efforts, marketing effectiveness, and the trends in the market. Sales reps use CRM as customer-focused technology that helps them devise strategies, which, in turn, helps them gain effectiveness in their selling methods. Notably, the best use of CRM system for sales reps will rest on the successful integration of the information acquired during data analysis over the course of their selling approach and practices. Another key area where accurate customer information will help salespeople tremendously is adaptive selling. In essence, the use of CRM technology will help sales reps in their efforts toward building and maintaining stronger customer relationships.

CRM *Value Proposition*

CRM solutions are offering fully functional, embedded workflow tools that are enabling firms to automate the greater part of regular, as well as unique, processes that are present among most customer-centric businesses. For example, CRM solutions make it possible to route a customer service request based on precedence or the nature of the case. A workflow can be established that sets off explicit actions or notifications based on the customer, the incident, or time-based conditions. Yet, despite the numerous benefits offered by CRM technology, it remains elusive to many firms. The primary reason for this elusiveness is that companies often focus only on the investment cost and ignore the CRM value proposition (Figure 1.3).

A manager needs to assess a CRM system from a broader perspective, as its domain is wide and it covers multiple business functions, such as marketing and analytics, customer service, integration of marketing and sales, and the like. Businesses may save money through separate or increment automation of customer-facing work processes and back-office applications; however, the value of CRM lies in the integration of these two facets of business operation. Additionally, CRM technology helps organizations offer better customer service, make call centers more

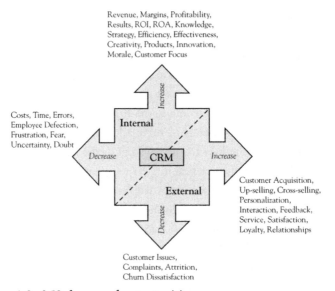

Figure 1.3. 360-degree value proposition.

efficient, cross-sell products more effectively, aid sales staff by closing deals faster, integrate marketing and sales processes, and discover new customers.

Current Market Environment

A recent research report by International Data Corporation (IDC), a global market intelligence firm, suggests that even in tough economic times such as now, spending on CRM software will increase. In the past, IDC had predicted $11.4 billion in CRM related applications sales in the year 2008. This phenomenon is not limited to developed industrial economies and big corporations. Medium-sized businesses that are members of the Association of Southeast Asian Nations spent more than $200 million in 2008, out of which $24 million came from CRM applications. SFA was the most adapted CRM module by medium businesses. These business trends cement the fact that organizations are increasingly exploring the potential of technology to develop, nurture, and sustain relationships with customers like never before.

In terms of CRM implementation, telecommunication and financial service industries are the leaders, while consumer goods manufacturers, retailers, and high technology companies are close behind them.

The findings of a survey of more than 1,600 business and IT professionals conducted by the Data Warehousing Institute highlight the fact that CRM budgets do not need to be extremely high; in fact, half of the respondents reported a CRM project budget of less than $500,000. In order to find the usefulness of CRM, Morgan Stanley surveyed 225 chief information officers and reported that 8% of respondents consider it critical, 20% think of it as useful, but only 38% think it reduces their IT budget. This suggests that businesses still have their doubts regarding CRM's value. Still, the growth of CRM technology has attracted several major companies to get into the business with PeopleSoft, Oracle, SAP, and Siebel, which are becoming key service providers. Linux, an open-source platform, is also getting a great deal of attention.

As a result of tough economic times, sales organizations are encountering severe challenges in maintaining the status quo. In order to survive, many sales organizations are trying new methods to leverage the eternal triangle that involves people, processes, and technology, and a CRM initiative is definitely one of the tools that sales organizations are increasingly relying on. A recent survey finding suggests a 33% increase in CRM usage by sales organizations from 2003 to 2008. Almost 90% of telesales teams are using CRM, and 1 in 3 organizations that are not currently using CRM technology stated an intention to do so in the upcoming years.

Availability and usefulness of CRM applications would make anybody think that with CRM, things must be going super smooth for sales organizations. Core CRM usage, however, is not directly proportional to sales effectiveness. As per the finding of the 2009 Sales Performance Optimization (SPO) study conducted by the chief sales officer (CSO) of Insights,[2] almost 63% of respondents reported that the primary goal of CRM initiatives was to increase revenue, yet only 16% of respondents witnessed revenue increases that would be attributed to CRM usage. It seems that CRM usage allowed sales reps to have more time to make more *average* sales calls; however, the necessity is that they need to make *great* sales calls. On the positive note, survey participants outlined the top three benefits they consider as outcomes of CRM system use: (a) improved salesperson-manager communications, (b) improved forecasting, and (c) reduced administrative burden on sales. Nonetheless, these benefits alone are not enough to justify the expense when considering the current tough economic situation.

Is CRM Good Only for Big Organizations?

There is also a widespread myth that CRM is only for big companies that have hundreds of employees and thousands of customers. The roots of this argument stem from very early examples of CRM implementation in big organizations because there were times when adoption of CRM was costly, and only companies that were financially strong and early adopters could decide to go for CRM. Yet, as time has passed, that is no longer a valid argument.

Smaller companies are increasingly adopting CRM as an integral part of their overreaching organizational strategy and piously implementing CRM systems. This is true not only for hosted CRM solutions but also for core CRM. A hosted CRM solution represents a situation where an organization outsources some, or all, of its CRM functions to a third-party supplier. The hosted CRM model is said to increase return on investment by decreasing costs and allowing a company to focus more resources on its main business areas. A core CRM program is typically housed internally, which allows for a greater level of customization but is also more expensive.

Recent research suggests that it is the smaller firms that drive the *new* growth in core CRM usage,[3] especially those who do not already have well-established CRM processes. Researchers conducting the SPO study find that approximately 68% of firms with 50 sales reps or fewer had a core CRM system in place. Notably, 5 years ago, this number was only 43%. On the other hand, application service providers (ASPs) penetrated the market because their solutions required less financial investment and were quickly implemented. According to a study by Nucleus Research, over 80% of companies that outsourced CRM achieved a positive return on investments. The study reported that problems with the traditional in-house CRM model include high software and consulting costs, ineffective user adoption, and poor management. However, because in-house CRM can be tailored more specifically to the particular needs of an organization, most larger companies opt for the traditional model.

Case 1. What Went Wrong at Cigna

New technology system implementation has its challenges, especially in the case of big corporations. Cigna Corporation's example outlines the risks involved in IT transformation. Cigna is one of the largest health insurers in the United States. The management at Cigna decided to move its 3.5 million customers from an old computer system to the new AS400 systems. The project was budgeted around $1 billion.

After working for several months on the preparation, Cigna moved all of its members to the new system in a matter of minutes. Unfortunately, at that time, they were unaware of the challenges that would soon threaten them. In a few months, Cigna was faced with problems on several fronts, resulting in unorganized customer services and revenue loss. A large group of customers, approximately 6% of its healthcare members, left the company, and hundreds of millions of dollars were reported as lost revenue.

A meticulous analysis of the whole project suggested that the unsuccessful restructuring of CRM systems and information technology at Cigna's health care unit was the key reason for this debacle. Glitches in the customer database system caused the misquotation of the number of customers by an extra 9,000,000. Problems raised the concern that Cigna's information system team even failed to understand the process, nonetheless the execution. The cost of implementing the project was much greater than what was expected, and the economic benefits that would emerge from the new system were wrongly assessed.

Source: Bass (2003).

CHAPTER 2

Technology Application Versus Business Strategy

Before we discuss the issues related to relationship strategy, let us go back to the basics and find out what "marketing" means and why there is focus on a new form of marketing, referred to as "relationship marketing."

The group of actual and potential buyers and sellers who come together to satisfy each other's needs and wants through exchange is an easy explanation of the term "market." Marketing is defined as a social and managerial process that helps individuals and organizations obtain what they need and want through creating and exchanging products and value with others. A customer need resembles a state at which a customer feels as though he or she is lacking something that could range from a physical or social need to an individual need. When a customer's need is influenced by society, culture, and individual lifestyle and values, it takes a specific form called "wants." Human *wants*, with or without *needs*, are combined with *buying power* to create a market demand for certain products or services. Organizations, through marketing processes, offer a mix of products, services, or experiences to buyers so that they can satisfy their needs and wants. This combination of offerings includes tangible products as well as activities and benefits that are not only intangible but also essential to fulfilling customers' needs. Unfortunately, firms frequently fall victim to "marketing myopia," which occurs when they are concerned only about the products or attributes they are selling. They more or less ignore the benefits and experiences that the product offers. In other words, they focus only on *what customers want* and ignore *what customers need*.

Changes in the marketplace, especially technological innovations, have tremendous effects on both firms and customers. Today's customers are informed, networked, and empowered like never before. As a result of the customer becoming the focal point of market-based exchanges, concepts such as relationship marketing and service dominant logic continue to draw attention from business and academia. The paradigm has shifted toward customer relationships, and marketing is better defined as *managing profitable relationships*. More and more organizations are adopting this approach by attracting new customers through better value offerings, and are not only maintaining the current customer base by raising satisfaction levels and tracking and keeping valuable customers but also are expanding their services to new customers.

Customers are very much concerned with a firm's value propositions—that is, the set of benefits that the organization promises to deliver to them in order to satisfy their needs. If customers perceive that the performance of the product or service is not matching up with their expectations, or they believe that the promise has not been delivered, they feel dissatisfied. To avoid such situations and to make customers happy, more and more firms are relying on relationship marketing, which prepares organizations to offer a single customer as many value propositions as possible instead of selling a single product to as many customers as possible. To execute the relationship marketing process, firms take different steps depending on their marketing goals and business types. The primary objectives, however, are to understand customer preferences, increase customer retention rates, develop products, modify messages based on customers' unspoken needs, and build positive customer experiences.

Devising a Strategy

Is a "Relationship Strategy" Right for You?

As many business people realize, in order to remain competitive in the marketplace, a firm needs to either play by the rules of the marketplace or create new rules. Before devoting all their resources and energy to build relationships, firms need to both revisit their goals and objectives as well as the goals and objectives of competitors and other players in the marketplace. Each market is unique in nature and imposes some limits. The most pragmatic approach for an organization is to evaluate the inside and outside environment, specifically the nature and purpose of exchanges, the goals and objectives of the organization and its competitors, and the resources capabilities of the firm.

The Relationship Spectrum

The relationship spectrum can be seen as a continuum, with transactional exchange at one extreme and relational exchange at the other. Anonymous transactions and routine or automated purchasing define the characteristics of transactional exchanges. Transaction-oriented firms give priority to short-term goals, and "making the sale" takes priority over most other considerations for the sales force. In this scenario, an individual salesperson will be interested only in his or her personal quota achievement. Interactions between a salesperson and customer are competitive instead of cooperative in nature. Information about customers is required; however, the firm uses this information for targeting and negotiations. Coordination between the customer and the firm is more or less limited to deliveries and contractual conditions.

Contrary to this, collaboration among, and integration of, all the channel partners, including the customer, is the key attribute of relational exchanges. Relationship-oriented firms practice long-term approaches, and "developing the relationship" takes priority over "making the sale." Their sales force is customer oriented, and interactions between a salesperson and customer are collaborative in nature. Information about the customer is utilized in finding needs and designing value propositions. Communication between buyer and seller resembles a joint problem-solving exercise, and coordination between them involves mutual commitments, trust, and shared incentives and goals.

Relational Capabilities

For an organization, it is not "just another task" to adapt and perform relationship strategy. It requires a market orientation, coordination among all functional units, integration of different processes, and relevant knowledge and skills. Becoming a market-oriented firm requires a common orientation that is disseminated throughout the entire organization and is completely assimilated within the organizational culture. By adopting this orientation, instead of focusing on short-term profits, the organization understands and focuses on the long-term value of each customer. Customers should become an integral part of the business process, and the firm should seek their involvement at every stage of the business processes. Moreover, these processes need to be aligned and executed in such a way that they link the organization to its customers. Additionally, customers should be motivated to interact with the organization and be provided with ways so that they can continuously do so. In addition, a central database needs to be generated and maintained where all the information related to customer interactions with each unit or individual is stored and accessible for strategy making. It is important that organizational or information silos are not created through the use of any technology or strategy that isolates one part of an organization from another, thus preventing the free flow of information.

Outlining Strategy

Outlining a relationship strategy that yields results is a complex task. An organization has to answer some critical questions related to their customers in order to come up with an effective strategy. To begin with, it is essential for the firm to think about what "loyalty" means to it as an organization, as no two organizations think about "loyalty" in the same way. One way for an organization to determine its meaning of "loyalty" is to find out the inputs as well as outputs needed to retain customers for a long time. Also, the firm needs to decide who its valuable and nonvaluable customers are, as it is not beneficial for the firm to try to retain nonvaluable customers. Firms also need to determine why customers defect from them or what the customers' primary reasons are for switching to a competitor. In order to connect with customers, firms will need to think about their interactions with customers. Specifically, a firm needs to determine what type of communication will motivate customers to interact with the firm and will strengthen their relationships. Additionally, firms also need to think about what types of information customer-contact employees require to benefit from customer relationships and maintain the value of the relationships.

An internal analysis that addresses these questions will help an organization devise a better relationship strategy. The task, however, is not complete even if a relationship strategy has been devised; the strategy needs constant attention and dedicated efforts for successful implementation and execution. Successful implementation of relationship strategy will require the firm to embrace "customer relationship" and "customer retention" as parts of its motto and to set objectives and goals accordingly throughout the organization. In addition, monitoring performance and collecting feedback to enhance performance is essential. Furthermore, realization of a strong relationship strategy will require partners both inside and outside the organization to internalize this philosophy. An organization's outside partners such as its suppliers, distributors, and other firms that are in alliance with the organization will have to coordinate their efforts toward customers. Inside the organization, all the functional units and their employees should be customer focused.

Because information about customers plays a critical role in developing and executing the relationship strategy, collection of such information should be the top priority for all employees and units. This information gathering should start with the existing customer base. For example, several retail chain stores collect information about customer buying habits and patterns by providing them with membership cards that give them discounts on store items every time they use it. From this data, firms learn who their heavy buyers are and then develop a plan to keep serving them well. Firms find this information helpful in retaining the best customers, and the customers are rewarded for their loyalty. Additionally, firms learn about defectors—those who stopped buying from them—and can try to win them back.

One great example of successful development and implementation of relationship strategy is the customer-oriented efforts that the office superstore Staples used to establish itself in the marketplace. As we all know, there were some common characteristics (low cost, self-service, wide variety, and high turnover) with other office superstores, and, very similar to convenience stores, there was little brand or store loyalty exhibited by customers. With the objectives of creating a loyal customer base and differentiating itself from competitors, Staples invested in developing a customer database that included exhaustive information about customers. With customer information in hand, Staples was able to spot heavy buyers, good customers, as well as defectors, which in turn enabled the company to target and serve useful user groups more effectively and, conclusively, made them loyal to Staples.

Staples' free membership card (Staples Rewards) helps the company to track customer buying patterns and provides them with customer information. It also brings smiles to customers' faces. For example, if a customer with a membership card brings an old ink cartridge back to the store, Staples gives the customer a $3 credit and 10% back in rewards on a new purchase.

Staples' focus on customer relationships and loyalty has proven successful over time. Even in the current economic recession, when more and more firms are filing for bankruptcy and losing profits, Staples enjoys a 26% increase in revenue, the addition of new stores, and expanding popularity of services such as copying and printing.[1] With effective customer relationship management (CRM) in place, Staples' website is one of the busiest sites in the world and helps offset any decline in retail sales.

Building Relationships Through CRM

Businesses are familiar with marketing management, which is the art and science of choosing target markets and building profitable relationships with them. Notably, the customer relationship concept has become the vital part of marketing management. The concept of the customer is not limited to finding out what customers a firm will serve or who is in their target market; instead, it focuses on how the firm can best serve the customers or what the firm offers in its value proposition. CRM technology can be helpful in realizing the customer concept by dividing the market into segments of customers, selecting the segments to cultivate, and building and maintaining profitable relationships with customers by delivering superior value to them.

A CRM system will enable a company to look at customers in a broader way and be vigilant about client-company interface throughout their network. Account-management operations can be taken to a completely new level. For example, an account manager who has a client in China will know exactly how her company's office in Japan is dealing with the client, enabling her to serve global customers in a more effective way. In addition, a global CRM system offers a much-improved way of communicating with account managers across the world.

In order to keep track of what is happening with a company's top clientele, account planning is very critical. A vital benefit of the CRM technology could be the detailed creation of a company's account plans. Account plans could be generated on an annual basis and may contain defined targets for each customer, thus setting a point of reference for accomplishment throughout the year. Establishing connections between CRM and a financial database, a company can feed information into their targets about new financial projections for the year. In addition, the management of price lists and product catalogs is possible with CRM, and complex pricing strategies are supported based on quantity or customer preferences.

CRM systems make it possible for businesses to record and maintain transactional customer interactions that are otherwise tough to keep track of. Transactional record keeping would compile a list of statements like "new customer enlisted in the database," "customer's problem resolved," "customer completed training course," and the like. Having such information available allows organizations to collect feedback on service satisfaction in a much better and efficient way.

The CRM system is very helpful to sales organizations. All the information related to customers can be stored in a single place, and sales representatives (hereafter, "sales reps") will no longer search for information that is distributed across various, distant homegrown systems. Sales reps will be better able to nurture and retain customers, track customers' growth, and share customer information with their colleagues. CRM systems can enable a sales team to conduct competitive analyses that include tracking and managing competitive profiling information, performing competitive comparisons based on user-defined criteria, and exhaustive win-loss breakdowns for each sale opportunity. Analysis can be done on an aggregated basis across the organization by competitor, territory, salesperson, product, or other measures. Sales managers will benefit, too, as they will have a tool for tracking performance at individual as well as at team levels, for setting benchmarks, and for the overall effective management of their sales force. At the highest level, top management will be better able to draw sales projections, outline strategies, and offer rewards.

CRM technology aids sales reps by managing information about a larger number of customers. Once equipped with such valuable information, sales reps are able to relate to customers without difficulty and can then be more responsive to critical issues, thereby shortening the duration of each sales encounter. They will also complete tasks with less effort. Additionally, with the help of CRM technology, customer cross-referencing will be easier among different departments within an organization, generating more sales potential and reducing efforts through evasion of multiple attempts geared toward the same prospective clients. Moreover, the overall sales process will be expedited, as CRM technology eases the processes of presale planning activities and improves the accuracy of sales forecasts.

Sales reps using CRM tools will find that analyzing customer data is not an overly complex and time-consuming process. They will be able to promptly focus on important information, which, in turn, will enable them to develop winning strategies in shorter time. The efforts and energy of sales reps will be preserved as CRM systems will help them gear up the process of strategy development and configuration of product offerings as per customer requisites. In addition, sales reps will be able to reduce their efforts by accelerating the formulation of relationship-building strategies, and decreasing the number of calls required to close a deal. They will also be able to significantly reduce the number of back orders.

It is a well-known fact that acquisition, analysis, and use of customer information are all particularly important for sales reps in demonstrating adaptive selling behaviors. CRM tools provide access to customer information that enables sales reps to improve or enhance their adaptive selling skills. A CRM system also aids sales reps in keeping track of customer purchase patterns and enables them to recognize prospects. Sales reps, with the help of CRM technology, will have decisive customer information that is essential for planning an effective sales encounter. Also, a CRM database provides opportunities to meticulously research customers and design sales presentations according to particular customer needs and wants. It is useful for keeping sales reps informed as well as for developing, implementing, or revising sales planning. Equipped with sound customer information, a salesperson better anticipates customer responses, prepares appropriate ways to meet customer needs, and overcomes customer objections.

Role of Technology in CRM

Clearly, technology is the backbone of CRM, and information technology's role in CRM is imperative and eminent. Without specially developed software applications, it would not be possible to realize a vibrant CRM strategy. This is because of the innovative software products that firms are able to use with CRM in order to sort through huge amounts of data. Technology tools are essential for collecting and analyzing customer information, which is needed to build relationships in the first place.

In terms of technology infrastructure requirements, over time, CRM packages have evolved tremendously. In comparison to past versions, current CRM packages are far more portable. There were times when an enterprise-level CRM package involved substantial investment related to technology infrastructure. Data centers can easily be deployed offshore, and growing global bandwidth allows companies to have complete solutions hosted anywhere in the world. Technological innovations have given organizations flexibility in terms of when, where, and how quickly they want to get going with CRM systems.

With the advancement of technology, businesses have to speed up their operations. Sales managers want to maintain instant monitoring of opportunity changes and pipeline trends. New applications help organizations to overcome the problems associated with CRM adoption by enhancing the value of information delivered to sales managers, sales operations, and sales representatives. Add-on applications build upon the existing CRM system to provide real-time views and understanding of how to improve sales operations, what data to collect, and how to measure performance. A complete visibility of the sales pipeline from suspect-prospect to customer-client is possible in real time. Applications keep detecting changing conditions in the sales pipeline, and reports are available through computer desktop applications as well as through mobile phones. With the help of advanced web technology, these add-on applications deliver a desktop application experience by being embedded directly into a user's core CRM application modules. Value delivery happens within the context of a user's existing workflow without any extra training.

CRM software and an accompanying strategy is increasingly becoming a necessity for sales organizations. As suggested by Jim Dickie, a partner with Chief Sales Officers Insight and a CRM expert, the *next* trend is not just implementing a CRM system but expanding current CRM functionality platforms. Complimentary applications and other sales force collaboration tools are setting the differentiation between effective and noneffective business styles. Applications such as WebEx and Live Meeting are supporting organizations in their efforts to conduct "webinars," virtual sales training, online demonstrations, and presentations for potential buyers. Salespeople and prospects may use them to meet virtually for almost all the aspects of the sales cycle, from introduction to final contract discussion. Sales reps can enhance effectiveness while keeping the costs low during sales encounters. For example, they can bring in technical staff or experts from their company to virtually meet the buyer and help them perform competitive analysis, needs analysis, handle objections, and address concerns. These applications are empowering salespeople, as they are no longer on their own; instead, they can leverage the full knowledge of their organization to help make a sales pitch.

Workflow Automation

With e-CRM infrastructure solutions, firms can replace their labor-intensive manual systems with workflow automation. This transformation should accelerate the speed of handling unique processes and maximize user productivity. The ultimate result would be increased employee effectiveness and reduced costs. The new CRM solutions are offering fully functional, embedded workflow tools, enabling firms to automate the greater part of regular, as well as exceptional, processes that are persistent among most customer-centric businesses. For example, it makes possible the routing of a customer service request based on precedence or nature of the case. A workflow can be established that sets off explicit actions or notifications based on customer, incident, or time-based conditions.

Pipeline Management

CRM systems allow organizations to notice what has been changed in the pipeline from one week to the next. However, the issue of tracking how a change has occurred remains unaddressed. Some companies have developed add-on applications for CRM solutions that can help in addressing this issue. Cloud9, for instance, offers an application that can locate what deals were won, lost, closed, or added to the company's pipeline. The Cloud9 Pipeline Accelerator Suite offers everything a sales organization would need to manage a dynamic pipeline, including report automation, and to complete sales pipeline visibility around the clock and around the world. Specifically developed for the customers of Salesforce.com (a hosted CRM solution company), the application's *role-based approach* empowers salespeople in very unique ways, such as delivering actionable viewpoints regarding historical trends and future predictions.

Content Management

A content management system is a tool that allows users to publish customized web pages, such as those outlining supporting business processes, sales cycle steps, or support policies. The goal is to synchronize a hosted CRM system with company-specific content that is otherwise kept on an intranet or in office files. It is an extremely helpful tool for supporting customer contact employees because it can be used for communicating policies, guidelines, and tips. For example, a user would be able to develop a rich and formatted web page guideline for salespeople concerning price discount policies. Users can also link this document to the opportunity management form within the same application. This would enable them to immediately access the information at any particular stage in the sales cycle.

Sales Knowledge Management

As an important category of CRM, sales knowledge management (SKM) provides sales organizations with a wealth of knowledge on potential customers. This knowledge about the buyer company, its executives, and financials can be decisive in creating a sales strategy. SKM capabilities enable salespeople to optimize their access to product data, sample proposals, and other presentation materials. Moreover, salespeople are able to share experiences from other colleagues who have had similar situations in the past. This union of CRM and sales processes is providing sales organization with a solid ground to work on. A greater access to the knowledge residing inside and outside of the organization has helped salespeople enhance their efficiency as well as effectiveness.

Lead Management

Taking on a new role as lead generator, salespeople are getting help from a lead generation system that could be integrated with a core CRM system. This application helps salespeople to get leads as well as research the prospects. There are several firms—such as Eloqua, Vrentz, and Marketo—that offer such applications to help salespeople plan, implement, and manage their own lead development and incubation campaigns.

Compensation Management

In the past, businesses performed compensation management with the help of shadow-accounting spreadsheets based in Excel. These practices are changing rapidly as new players enter into the arena. Firms such as Centive, Callidus, and Varicent offer applications to model, execute, and optimize incentive management programs. With the help of these applications, firms are better able to direct the sales operations in the right direction.

While discussing the role of technology in CRM, one key point has to be mentioned. This is that executives are often engulfed in hardware and software issues or IT infrastructure before considering the primary business drivers, and, eventually, they lose track of the objectives of the project. Focusing on the technology needs of a CRM initiative before outlining a relationship strategy could be lethal to organizations. Devising a relationship strategy and developing a business case for CRM is far more important than arranging the technology tools to enable it.

Project leaders and senior management need to make sure that in a CRM initiative, primary responsibility should fall on the shoulders of the sales, marketing, and customer service units. Information technology departments should work as key partners in the process. After all, CRM is more about the customers than the technology that enables it. If there is a well-developed strategy in place, collaboration and compromise among different departments participating in a CRM initiative will be possible, which is very critical for a successful CRM implementation. Considering the global nature of today's business environment, it is highly critical to have a well-developed strategy before technology investment. For example, during mid-1990s, GE Capital initiated ambitious efforts to develop a central database for all of its global subsidiaries and units. Even though the company employed innovative technology tools and techniques, the idea did not go very far. One of the problems they faced was dealing with privacy regulations for foreign consumers that limited the information export. Another hurdle was how to interpret the data without having grassroots knowledge of the local culture and consumer preferences. This example underscores the fact that even the best of the technology cannot be of great help if a well-planned strategy is not in place.

Case 2. CRM Transformation at Host.net

Company Background

U.S.-based Aplicor Inc. has been providing subscription-based and hosted CRM and ERP solutions to businesses since 1999. Aplicor's business approach puts emphasis on the value of actually leveraging CRM information by focusing on business process automation over data storage and analysis, and business intelligence over traditional reporting.

Host.net, a U.S.-based broadband company, operates in the highly competitive market of Internet and network services providers. In this market, success requires businesses to concentrate on operational excellence because most companies offer very similar services, such as web hosting and IP phone service.

Problem

Host.net was aware of the fact that in such a competitive market, operational excellence would rely on communication and the timely flow of information. The company recognized that front- and back-end operations needed integration. For example, sales initiatives should be coordinated with back-end operations and customer incidents reported at back-end must be conveyed to salespeople. To address these issues, Host.net, which was already a customer of Aplicor CRM, decided to initiate an effort to transform the existing CRM arrangements that primarily support data capturing to a system that would positively influence the company's processes.

Solution

Workflow automation emerged as the early challenge to the Aplicor team. In some cases, the working of existing processes was very ambiguous, or there were no clear guidelines for a work process. The Aplicor team worked closely with Host.net management and project members to find appropriate solutions. The problems were resolved by synchronizing Aplicor's content management and workflow engines with Host.net's specific business processes.

Aplicor Content Management enables rich-text pages to be developed and connected to processes within the Aplicor solution set. For example, sales opportunities are coupled with multistage sales cycles, and customer service incident profiles contain service-level agreement details. This provides employees with direct access to the corporate guidelines for solution selling and service standards from compliance. Some other pages include prospecting techniques, standard operating procedures, and best practices in marketing.

Aplicor has set up workflow as an enterprise tool supported via a CRM system. Aplicor's workflow is both a tool kit and a set of standard business processes. If requirement emerges, additional workflows can be created to match organizational, industry, or department-specific needs. Host.net started using Aplicor workflow for several key functions, such as sending operational notifications to concerned groups when a prospect is moved to the negotiation stage in the sales process to improve operational lead time. In another example, workflow is being used for notifying a salesperson of all high priority cases that were reported to support division.

Source: Pombriant (2005).

CHAPTER 3

The Role of the Customer in Technology and Strategy Implementations

Developing and implementing a relationship strategy is not an overnight task. In addition, it is nonpragmatic to expect the results from such strategy, if in place, all of the sudden. It is a long process that takes consistent organizational efforts. During this journey, customers' roles changes multiple times, and their relationship with the company evolves. The journey of customer relationship building goes through several milestones, such as customer-centric activities, customer acquisition, retention, loyalty, and so on. Now, the vital question for organizations is, *how does customer relationship management help achieve these milestones?*

To address this issue, first, a firm needs to understand their customers in the context of customer relationship management (CRM). It is evident that firms invest in CRM technology because they wish to be able to differentiate between profitable and nonprofitable customers, offer customized services, and hold on to profitable customers for a long time. In order to get the most out of CRM technology, however, a firm has to develop and maintain a customer-centric approach throughout its operations. Consistent with the guidelines of relationship marketing, a value system that considers the relationship with the customer to be an asset needs to be in place within an organization. Such a customer-centric management system would comprise of structural facets ensuring that the organizational approach and actions are based on customer needs rather than on internal functional mechanisms.

Ever-changing market conditions and increasing offerings have made it challenging for organizations to remain competitive. One reliable prescription is that a business should track and detect customer preferences and make business adaptations accordingly. In addition, along with innovation, customer integration is one of the best sources of differentiation. Notably, CRM tools and technology are enabling companies to keep their fingers on the pulse of their customers. Technological innovations have made it possible to find and serve customers better, but it has also made them vulnerable, as a customer is just *"one click away"* from their competition. In response, in hopes of becoming more efficient, companies are trying hard to automate the facets of their customer relationships using customized or packaged software solutions. To serve customers more effectively, firms are relying on software applications that reorganize and reorient the databases so that relevant customer data are easily available.

For organizations, it is a well-known fact that acquiring a new customer is a much more costly affair than retaining an existing one. A research study published in *Harvard Business Review* reports that most of the organizations lose half of their customers in just 5 years, and that certain companies can actually enhance their profits by almost double if they can retain 5% more of their customers. It seems natural to believe that customers who had experienced problems with a specific organization are less probable to become loyal to that organization in comparison with those who have not experienced problems with that organization. Interestingly, however, the probability of becoming loyal to the given organization goes way up if customers had experienced problems but their problems were handled appropriately. In terms of cost-effectiveness, technology is the best way to resolve a customer issue or answer a customer query relative to phone support or e-mail.

In the following section, we specifically discuss the three significant aspects of customer relationships: customer satisfaction, retention, and loyalty. Today's customers are empowered, informed, and networked like never before, and it is critical for firms to have outlined strategies if they desire to function in this new consumer-centric marketplace and to acquire, satisfy, and retain them. Furthermore, the organization should have separate customer-specific strategies related to each of these aspects.

Customer Acquisition

In the end, a salesperson's performance relies on his or her ability to identify potential customers, learn about their needs, and assess their value.

It is essential for salespeople and firms to acquire as many new customers as possible in the early stage of their business' life-span. It has been argued that salespeople's role has evolved from sales makers to customer creators. The importance of developing a qualified prospect base to cope with customer attrition has always been high, but the emergence of CRM has enabled salespeople to execute the prospecting process in a very different fashion.

CRM technology has made it easy to keep track of customers' movements through the sales cycle. For example, Cisco Inc. uses a CRM system from Salesforce.com that enables them to effectively manage prospects. CRM tools such as dashboards, account planning, and partner reports are very helpful in this process. Cisco's salespeople monitor lead conversion rates, account plans, accounts profitability, and account opportunities with the help of dashboards. Moreover, in a team-selling scenario, other members, as well as the manager, can collaborate through the CRM database to formulate or sharpen the sales strategies aimed at converting a prospect to a customer. A CRM pipeline dashboard, a tool to manage relationships in the pipeline or sales funnel, provides the sales team with active updates as potential customers move through the pipeline. The CRM pipeline framework classifies potential customers as per their location in the sales process, which keeps salespeople informed regarding prospects and expected revenue details. Finally, the dashboard helps salespeople plan accordingly in order to achieve sales quotas.

CRM systems provide good resources for storing and accessing sales information, including basic data such as customer name, contact, and address, as well as complex data (e.g., past purchases, product preferences, buying-center members' details, forecasted sales, future sales opportunities). Notably, these rich sales data reside in a shared CRM database, making it easier for other sales force members to access and utilize this data while planning sales strategies. Today's customers are faced with a plethora of information and thus crave relevancy in marketing communications. Customers do not want to be overloaded by irrelevant data. CRM tools and techniques make *relevant marketing communications* possible. At the macro level, CRM enables marketers to be consistent while communicating with customers irrespective of channel, location, and time. At the micro level, a salesperson can optimize interactions with prospects. A properly managed CRM database enables salespeople to review the background of a prospect so that the salesperson is very focused while meeting with the prospect—not only on the topics related to their business and industry but also on a more personal and social level.

Customer Satisfaction

It seems intuitive for organizations to keep customers happy, and one would imagine that these organizations would surely have a plethora of satisfied customers. However, the truth is that two-thirds of customers do not feel valued by the firms serving them. For the organization, unfortunately, it is difficult to track down such customers, as only 1 out of 25 dissatisfied customers will convey their dissatisfaction directly to the concerned firm. Nevertheless, they will spread the bad word among their peers, friends, relatives, and even to complete strangers, thanks to the World Wide Web. In fact, dissatisfied customers discuss their bad experiences with approximately 9 to 12 people, in comparison to satisfied customers, who talk to only 4 or 5 people about their positive experiences. Some specific benefits of satisfied customers are that they tend to stay with the organization longer, they are less sensitive to prices, and they spread positive experiences by word of mouth and recommend firm's products to others.

It is not a complex puzzle to understand that satisfied customers are good for organizations. Salespeople should deal with existing customers with the same degree of diligence and responsiveness as they would in dealing with new customers. As existing customers can easily churn, or switch, from one supplier to another, they are much better prospects than new leads who salespeople have not yet met. Similarly, satisfied existing customers are the best source of new customers. Oftentimes, they are termed as *supplementary salespeople*, who can enhance the inflow of new prospects through positive word of mouth and referrals.

Significant issues to consider are how to make customers happy and what role CRM technology should play in making them happy. Generally, customer satisfaction with a product or service depends on perceived value, which is the customer's evaluation of the difference between all the benefits and costs of a marketing offer relative to those of competing offers. A customer will feel satisfied if the product's performance, as perceived by the customer, is greater than his or her expectations of the product. In a market-oriented environment where the customer is central to business, satisfying the customer may require unique approaches. Customers place importance on "experiences" over "products" and expect personal attention from each unit and employee of the organization they are dealing with. Customers are willing to share their personal information with the firm in order to get a customized solution, but they also want their privacy to be respected and secured. In maintaining the privacy and security of their financial and personal information, customers are becoming cautious of companies' data collections efforts, which are essential in maintaining and supporting CRM solutions. Firms that intend on developing a sophisticated CRM database should consider security and privacy as high priority issues and should clearly convey their intentions to customers. Customers should be allowed to opt out of a program depending on their own priorities. CRM provides the comprehensive view of the customer, hence paving the way for sales, product development, and marketing to take tactical and strategic actions that can satisfy customer needs while respecting their privacy, maintaining security, and enhancing relevancy.

The proper handling of customer expectations after closing a sale is not a stand-alone task for a salesperson. It will require a strategic plan and collaborative efforts by the larger organization. People from various units, such as shipping and inventory, information technology, customer support, and so on should support their salespeople. CRM technology provides firms with new ways to shape, enhance, and extend partnership-oriented communications with their customers by enabling all the units to update, access, and utilize customer information. With a centralized database in place, and each unit connected to the database, information flow is smooth and transparent.

Customer Retention

As competition increases and profit margins shrink, losing "profitable" customers can result in severe consequences for an organization. Customer attrition not only results in loss of revenue but also loss of time and money that was invested in gaining the customers in the first place (see Figure 3.1). It has been argued that the cost of acquiring a new customer is usually 5 to 10 times greater than the cost of retaining current

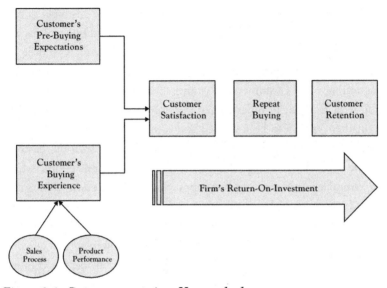

Figure 3.1. *Customer retention: How and why.*

customers. High retention results in a larger customer base. Moreover, in certain industries and markets, customer retention is crucial for survival. For example, an average online business needs to gain three purchases in order to break even after acquiring a new customer. Notably, understanding the needs and wants of customers has been touted as the best way of retaining them.

A scenario where a customer shuts off his or her business is not a good situation for an organization; however, the worst news is when a customer leaves a business for one of its competitors. Finding out why a customer selects a competitor can help the organization retain customers in the future. Firms should study the characteristics of buyers and the circumstances under which they decide to switch in order to predict the switching behavior of other customers and to sort out customers who are worth investing time and effort in. Another objective is to find the best approaches, such as promotions or deals, to prevent customers from switching.

Expanding and retaining business and relationships with customers provide salespeople with several opportunities, such as cross-selling, full-line selling, and up-selling. For example, full-line selling—that is, recommending products and services related to the primary product sold to the customer—can be a method of value offerings for salespeople. In another example, salespeople who have established strong relationships with customers and are aware of their needs can start selling products (i.e., cross-selling) that are not directly related to the primary product bought by the customer. Such expansion selling techniques bring revenue to the firm and also make things easier for buyers, as they do not have to deal with different suppliers for their different needs; in turn, the business retains customers for a long time.

Importantly, not all customers bring profits to the organization; therefore, retaining *profitable customers* is the key to success. The concept of the customer life cycle (CLC) is helpful to organizations in understanding this practice. The CLC is made up of multiple stages that occur during the relationship between a customer and an organization. Some of the critical stages in the CLC are prospects (i.e., potential customers making up the target market for an organization); responders (i.e., potential customers who are showing some interest by responding to the firm's marketing communications); profitable customers (i.e., current customers who are contributing to the firm's profit); and, nonprofitable customers (i.e., current customers who are using the firm's products but not contributing in profits may be because they incur high costs). For businesses, it is important to track CLC events, and CRM can be helpful in doing so. Through data mining of a comprehensive database, CRM can help determine customer behaviors and tendencies surrounding different life cycle events. Price-sensitive customers frequently switch suppliers to take advantage of the "best deals" from competing firms. Data mining can be used for identification of customer characteristics, which, in turn, enables a firm to focus on those customers who will produce the profit in the long run.

Other similar ideas, such as customer lifetime value (CLV), are also supported by CRM and need to be discussed when deciding on valuable customers. CLV is defined as the total purchases that the customer would make in the due course of customer lifetime. The combined total of all CLVs for a company represents its customer equity. The basic building blocks of CRM enable organizations to manage and use the knowledge they have about their customers to understand and keep track of CLV and overall customer equity. More importantly, CRM systems can help organizations profile customers so that they can optimize resource allocation and utilization while retaining customers. For example, Barclays, a global financial services provider serving a diverse base of customers and clients, adopted a value-based management program to synchronize decision making at all levels in the organization. Under this program, the management introduced a value-aligned performance measurement tool to help the sales unit identify valuable customers and take appropriate actions to enhance profitability and create shareholder value. The company utilized the information received through the customer value measurement tool to facilitate managerial decision making and to support value-based sales incentives.

Businesses need to understand that not all customers are worth retaining. It is also critical, however, to explore possibilities of turning a currently nonprofitable customer into a profitable one through some investments. CRM technology permits organizations to perform *customer profiling* that can help address some of these critical issues. Technology can help organizations construct socioeconomic behavioral profiles of customers. These profiles can help to outline customer progression. Moreover, a customer profile is useful for analyzing a customer's present value and for applying different criteria in order to predict future business potential in encouraging or discouraging retention efforts. After tracking down qualified customers, the organization can plan to create and deliver better value and positive experience to customers.

Customer Loyalty

Facing tough competition and a challenging economy, businesses seek to convert occasional buyers into loyal customers in order to maintain customer spending at a standard level. Most firms have already implemented, or are at least thinking of implementing, formal loyalty initiatives. The purpose is to attract, convert, and keep existing customers. Having a loyal customer base helps an organization in several dimensions, such as reduction in costs and an increase in profits. It has been argued that a customer's average purchase amount increases over time (e.g., an average of 9% in the insurance business), thus bringing in more revenue. In addition, a loyal customer base facilitates cost reductions through reducing sales cycles, accelerating order processing, and increasing customer referrals.

CRM technology can facilitate a sales organization's ability to sustain strong relationships with customers and earn their loyalty (see Figure 3.2). Sales forces using CRM technology are able to increase service quality by demonstrating responsiveness and reliability. By enhancing storage and retrieval of key customer concerns and other relevant details, CRM technology can influence the reliability component of service quality. Also, salespeople are able to quickly access important information about order processing and shipping, for example, which, in turn, conveys the message of "being responsive" to customers. With a CRM system in place, salespeople are able to access a broad organizational memory base containing other employees, departments, and databases. This helps them to update their approach and knowledge about business relationships.

Some organizations may find themselves in a situation where they have already been incorporating customer satisfaction and loyalty measures into business practices. It is possible, however, that an organization's current methodology does not provide all the insights required to gain the absolute potential of customer value measurement. This type of organization needs the best possible combination of the many options for

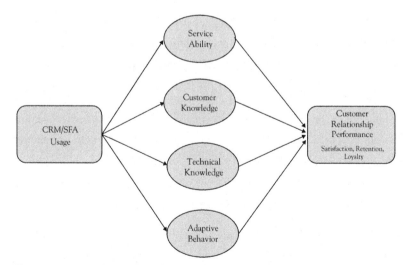

Figure 3.2. Mediating mechanism for customer satisfaction, retention, and loyalty.

Source: Aherane, Jones, Rapp, and Mathieu (2008).

transforming customer perceptions. Such efforts will optimize the use of the company's resources, minimize the invasion on customer's time, and add value for both the company and customers. Yet, oftentimes, management ends up following a "more of the same" routine as key process owners inside the company have become familiar with the current system and have achieved a comfort level over time. These people do not want to receive information in any other format and therefore avoid, and sometimes even oppose, any changes.

Having perfect information available about its customers all the time is almost impossible for an organization; however, this knowledge can be continuously enhanced through the use of CRM dynamics. CRM should be seen as a continuous learning process for an organization. CRM technology, with its storing, accessing, and networking functions, will enable and facilitate collection, dissemination, and utilization of customer information. Therefore, salespeople will be able to enhance their knowledge of customer needs, interests, and dislikes.

As we have discussed before, rich and positive interactions between the buyer and seller shape the strength and longevity of their business relationship. Companies aware of this fact are increasingly focusing on making each customer experience a memorable one. Such customer experiences are providing firms with opportunities to affect customer acquisition, satisfaction, retention, and loyalty. CRM tools and technology can help organizations to take such relationships to a new level. With a proper CRM system in place, organizations are better able to manage customer experiences and successfully engage loyal customers to evangelize their brands. CRM has given a new boost to the *customer evangelism* phenomenon, which is described as enabling loyal customers to become a volunteer sales force. Such evangelists create not only financial benefits for the company but also social benefits.

Loyalty Scheme Outsourcing

A new trend has emerged recently where firms are outsourcing their loyalty schemes. For example, Sainsbury's, a UK-based retail chain, dropped its in-house loyalty scheme and signed up Nectar, which is a multiple-member rewards club. Some other members of the club include British Petroleum and Homebase. The Nectar program is owned and operated by Loyalty Management UK Limited. After becoming registered members, shoppers can collect Nectar points on their everyday shopping and then spend them in other places. Nectar's management claims that this approach is better than in-house loyalty schemes, as shoppers have the opportunity of earning points with several different companies. Moreover, shoppers can accumulate more points in less time. For example, an average household of 4 members can save enough points in 3 months to get 3 return flights from London to Paris.

Critics of this practice argue that members of such schemes are not loyal to individual retailers or businesses, as their loyalty resides within Nectar. Proponents, on the other hand, argue that individual retailers get access to large databases at a reasonable cost. Additionally, business partners can target potential customers who are currently dealing with other institutions, whereas the companies who have the in-house loyalty scheme can only utilize the existing customer base.

Case 3. Tesco's Loyalty Card Scheme: A Success Story

Focusing on benefits from customer loyalty programs is not a very new phenomenon; however, the percentage of companies that are doing it is low. Tesco, a leading retailing company in the United Kingdom, has successfully reaped benefits from its customer loyalty program. In 1995, Tesco's growth and customer service priorities motivated the management to undertake CRM initiatives. The example of Tesco's loyalty card scheme helps to understand how the information collected through CRM tools can be used to transform a firm's marketing strategies and gain benefits in the long run.

Started as a trial scheme, club cards were offered to customers at a few selected Tesco stores. Analyzing the sample data collected from 14 stores running the Clubcard trial, the company's marketing specialists were able to extract insightful information. One of the most interesting insights to emerge was that the majority of Tesco's profit was coming from the minority of customers. The management was able to recognize and appreciate the economic significance of these loyal customers. For example, one store manager invited 300 customers to the store for a meeting and greeting over breakfast. Another store manager wrote personal letters to shoppers, apologizing for any inconvenience due to store remodeling. The response from customers was much better than in other cases where a store would put the ad and apology in a local newspaper. When the results of this trail scheme were presented in a board meeting, the chairman, Sir Ian MacLaurin, told the marketing team, "What scares me about this is that you know more about my customers in 3 months than I know in 30 years."

Whereas other retailers were happy knowing how much each customer spent in each department and then sending out similar discount coupons to everyone, Tesco's marketing efforts were very focused and cost-effective. Through advanced statistical techniques, each shopper's cart was analyzed by scoring each product against multiple dimensions. For example, product origin (domestic or foreign), brand, price range, and so on. This information was then fed into a clustering model, which identified different customer segments, such as health-focused, price sensitive, and the like. In simple words, Tesco was able to outline its shoppers' needs and accordingly tailor its products and services. Four out of six discount vouchers sent to cardholders were for goods that customers already purchased, whereas the remaining two were for related items. Based on customers' shopping profiles, Tesco was able to figure out what ranges in nonfood items are most likely to appeal to shoppers.

Instead of returning dividends to customers in the form of discount coupons, Tesco planned to exchange those for information on its shoppers' purchase patterns. The company signed up numerous Clubcard partners and was selling points to other companies such as Marriot and Nationwide, for example. Interestingly, these partners can pass the points on to their customers; however, Tesco Clubcard vouchers are only good for Tesco stores.

Some challenges and criticisms of this loyalty scheme emerged. Over a period of several years (1995–2002), Tesco let the £1 billion of profits go by delivering cash back to its customers, as a gesture of appreciation, through discount coupons. However, in the long run, the scheme proved to be a successful phenomenon, garnering millions of pounds of profit and enabling Tesco to become the market leader. Banking on the customized information, Tesco saved money by using direct mail and dropping most of its TV advertisements. With millions of households as active members, Tesco was turned into a customer-centric organization. Membership gave customers a stake in the company and another reason to shop at Tesco.

Sources: Humby, Hunt, and Phillips (2004); Mesure (2003, October 10).

CHAPTER 4

Selection Decision Process and Research

Customers are becoming more reliant on e-commerce to capture the best value, as globalization and Internet technologies have connected all the corners of the world. In little time, a customer can explore a firm's four P's (product, place, price, and promotion) and compare them in an easily accessible global marketplace. Firms try to maintain a customer-oriented image throughout the world, possible only through a standard customer relationship management (CRM) methodology. Web-based CRM applications are also extremely helpful for effective and efficient global account management. No organization can implement and execute a relationship strategy without coordinated interdepartmental teamwork, which is made possible by technology tools that help develop and maintain a centralized customer database.

Representing this trend, CRM spending has emerged as a major piece of the information technology investment in organizations. Efforts to better serve customers are not necessarily reflected in customer service operations. The majority of the firms think that once their CRM software is installed, all of their customer-related issues are resolved and successful implantation of CRM is complete. However, this kind of thinking ignores two of the most critical issues: selection of an appropriate CRM package based on the organization's needs and the firm's existing culture. When moving toward a technology solution, there must be a drastic change in terms of how an organization thinks about the customer, executes processes, rewards and evaluates employees, and uses metrics to analyze performance.

Depending on the type of business a firm is engaged in, such as service offering or product manufacturing, CRM will be utilized very differently. In such cases, CRM suppliers need to offer CRM applications that differ in terms of scope and functionality. For example, a service company will need a vendor that provides software solutions that are specific to professional services. It is highly unlikely that a firm will halt all other processes and projects that are already in place to provide space for a CRM project. As a new addition to the family, a CRM project needs to be well integrated with other business processes such as a firm's financial management system or inventory-management system. Such goals can only be achieved through a meticulous evaluation of the internal and external environments of an organization.

Internal Assessment

Choosing a CRM software solution can easily become a hassle if not undertaken properly. To save time and money, some organizations even hire a consultant to aid in this crucial decision (see case study at the end of this chapter for an example). Intermediary parties, such as software sellers, can also advise on this issue, but their personal biases may interfere with an organization making a choice suitable to its own specific needs. Nevertheless, the best advice is to do some in-house research and analyze options that synchronize with the organization's internal needs. However, it is important to mention that the concerned company should not be trapped with an option that may sound attractive but that is of no use to that specific company. For example, every business wants to have the ability to customize their product, but, pragmatically, not every business can do this, as it requires resources and investment. At the same time, the company should not settle with a very narrow solution just to save on resources and investments. The company needs to maintain a broader perspective so that their technology remains on the cutting edge, which is essential in today's global competitive marketplace. The price tag of the product is another main issue to consider. It is highly recommended that an organization has detailed information concerning the complete costs of the project, including costs that may originate from implementation delays, downtime in current operations, training costs, licensing costs, annual maintenance costs, and costs of additional modules.

Finally, companies should be aware that there is no one, universal CRM package that applies to all business types and needs. The selection of an appropriate and compatible CRM package is extremely important for firms to reap benefits from CRM technology. The selection depends on the features of the business itself—for example, business size, nature of products and services, and the frequency of marketing communications. There are several CRM applications to choose from, each of which is characterized by different dimensions that may apply to different types of businesses. An exhaustive scanning of the organization's needs and internal environment is necessary before deciding which one is appropriate for the business.

Scope

It is very important for an organization to carve out its priorities and finalize a scope for its CRM project. Project scaling enables project teams to prioritize activities and modify functionality during deployment of the system. In addition, with a defined scope, a project team will have a clear understanding of distinct requirements and implementation expectations. Once the scope is clear, it will be much easier to construct a project strategy that reflects a firm's resource requirements, such as technology tools and skilled labor, required tasks, and overall time frame.[1]

CRM applications range from basic contact management solutions to high-end packages that interface with inventory systems and accounting packages, providing firms with details of their past transactions with customers, suppliers, employees, and assembly units. The technology solution selected hinges on the core functions of a business and the role of the customer in the buying experience. For example, customers buying convenience goods in local grocery stores do not look for a unique shopping experience and do not expect the store to have information about their likes and dislikes. Therefore, customer expectations involved in the business transactions of the organization should determine, in part, the scale of CRM technology investments.

Organizations thinking about adopting CRM systems have two main models to choose from: (1) core, or on-premise, CRM solutions, and (2) application service provider (ASP), or hosted, CRM solutions.

Core CRM system providers include big enterprises such as Microsoft, Oracle, and SAP. Many big organizations and early adopters of CRM systems have chosen this model. In addition, some organizations develop in-house applications that can offer basic services such as territory management, pipeline management, lead management, opportunity management, and sales forecasting. A company interested in this mode would be required to purchase software at the beginning of the implementation process. The company also has to pay license fees based on per-user figures. The next step would be the implementation of the system. Implementation itself requires separate investments in terms of hardware and other infrastructure resources, and sometimes its cost runs higher than the licensing fees. Finally, the company would be responsible for establishing and sustaining an organizational environment conducive to CRM.

The second option that takes the software-as-a-service approach requires a recurring annual or monthly per-user payment. Most of these options do not require infrastructure investments, and support functions are outsourced to the solution provider. Systems can either be installed on a customer's own servers or accessed through the hosting provider's servers via the Internet. Recently, some vendors who maintain a standard, underlying data model have started offering hybrid solutions.

Both approaches have their strengths and limitations, and a buyer's decision to select either of the models would depend on the company's context and priorities. Core CRM providers argue that hosted solutions cost more than on-premise solutions in the long run. On the other hand, the financial risk for the buyer is relatively greater in the case of the on-premise models. Perhaps a hosted CRM solution would permit a company to concentrate on core issues, as most of the supporting functions are outsourced to an ASP. However, this aspect of the process typically fuels an organization's concern over the security of its data.

Arguably, defining the scope of a CRM project is often a daunting task. One major issue that requires attention is the decision concerning who should be in charge of scaling the CRM project in the first place. Internal conflicts among departments and executives, due to different objectives and work styles, are common in any organization. Decisions regarding the scope of a CRM system can be affected by such unresolved tensions. Because of their close proximity to customers, it is often the marketing division and business development executives that take the lead in scaling the project.

Determining the scope of a CRM project will have more clarity if analysis of the current system and work process has been completed. For example, if a company has already established a rigorous customer-data collection process, the future CRM system should be more sophisticated in applications related to data analysis than those in data gathering. As suggested by Jill Dyché, a CRM expert, optimum scaling requires the clear understanding of several key points:

- Particular tools and techniques that will be used in CRM implementation
- Required workforce and skills to implement the project
- Number of trainers and consultants needed to enhance users' skills
- A pragmatic period needed to finish the first phase
- Organizational perimeter, limitations, and potential political problems

Finally, outlining the scope of a CRM project will require an unyielding decision from the organization on how much customer information they want to collect and to what extent they want to explore it. The amount of information can definitely be adjusted, but there should be no compromise on the completeness of data. Notably, different modules of CRM system offer distinct notions about customers. A good CRM system should provide the company with different aspects of customer information so that a big picture is possible. A company may also want to decide if they want a CRM system for the whole organization or only for units that would benefit the most from it. Consequently, the organization can expand and implement CRM in other divisions.

Functionality

There are several types of CRM packages available in the marketplace that serve different purposes. In order to get help from a CRM solution and to construct positive customer experiences, an organization needs to look for a package that has attributes relevant to its business structure. Above all, a company's solution should be designed to yield significant increases in customer service, loyalty, margins, and revenue. Binary Spectrum, based in Bangalore, India, designs and develops customized CRM solutions. The company's success is based on the practice of keeping the particular needs and requirements of an organization or an industry on the forefront while deciding on the functionalities of a CRM package. For example, the company's retail solutions incorporate functionalities designed to face retail industry's challenges such as faster checkout process, dynamic promotions and discounts, optimal inventory management, and access and efficiency of after-sales service.

An effective CRM solution enables an organization to manage every stage of a customer life cycle starting from lead generation to finally servicing the sale. To facilitate the operations at different stages of the customer life cycle, a typical CRM system includes different dimensions such as marketing, sales, and service, which serve different purposes at different stages. Therefore, three general types of CRM packages that are most relevant to any business operation are marketing automation systems, sales force automation (SFA), and customer service automation systems.

When deciding on the customer service functionalities of a CRM solution, a company should keep in mind that the package must allow the company to be adaptable enough to sustain itself in a constantly evolving market environment. Tools that can help companies consistently analyze their customer support performance through organized and continuous feedback from customers will be on the priority list. For example, the support team should be able to retain and manage a case history so that they can review past interactions and get to the bottom of any issues.

Marketing Automation

In a given organization, the marketing division is primarily responsible for developing, targeting, executing, and analyzing campaigns. Such campaigns are run through multiple communications channels and target a predefined set of potential customers. The campaign's execution involves the communication of a particular message regarding an individual product or a group of products, a service, or the company in general. Performance analysis involves the selection of qualitative (subjective) as well as quantitative (objective) measures for a given period and the monitoring of those measures. In general, the marketing division is responsible for generating momentum in the marketplace and for interacting with customers. All of these actions require proper planning, which in turn requires appropriate and relevant information.

Marketing works alongside the sales division, and, thus, an important objective of the marketing package of a CRM system is to generate sales leads. These leads are fed into the sales process and ultimately contribute to sales revenue. One of the key outcomes of a marketing campaign is leads generation. However, extracting the hot leads from the information collected throughout the campaign is a tough task and requires a lot of work. The lead management function can be a helpful tool, as it deals with every aspect of lead generation.

Sales Force Automation

The sales functionalities of the CRM package are designed to supply an organization's sales force with the tools, information, and opportunity to better manage and execute sales processes. As discussed in the marketing automation section, a CRM system will provide salespeople and managers information on customer interactions, leads, and other opportunities that will help in achieving their sales goals. Considering the fact that sales representatives' jobs are not in-house jobs, as they spend most of their time in the marketplace, an SFA package would be beneficial to them, as it would allow them to instantly access corporate information from anywhere.

SFA is helpful at every stage of a sales cycle. For example, it organizes all the information regarding prospects, including expected budget, spending trends, the potential decisions makers, and expected dates for making the decision. Analysis can be performed to make sure that sales representatives are investing their time and energy in the most likely and pragmatic deals.

Customer Service Automation

With the Internet being used by so many people, customers have many ways to interact with companies. This becomes a challenge for businesses, as it is difficult to keep track of all the touch points. An effective customer service automation package can enable a firm to monitor and capture all interactions with all customers despite the different touch points. The basic function of this application involves the managing of customer service. Some of the typical customer service–related functionalities involve the management of service orders, service contracts, planned services, warranties, service level agreements, resources and workforces, call-center operations, and service knowledge. The renowned software company SAP offers a service management application with a CRM package specially designed for high-technology companies that are specifically looking for service automation functionality. The service management application enables businesses to deliver effective customer support through several advanced applications and tools, such as service planning and administration, transactional support, and financial analytics.

Organization Culture

There are many times when a firm initiates changes that impact its internal culture, and it is important to recognize that the implementation of a CRM solution will be one of those changes. Many times, when a change is implemented that affects the culture of an organization, the objectives of the proposed initiatives are often not met. Therefore, a firm that incorporates a CRM strategy needs to take a deeper look inside the organization's culture and assess its ability to adapt to new initiatives. Strong support from a firm's executives and a clear, long-term plan are the very basic ingredients of this process.

A prolific researcher in the field, Edgar H. Schein, describes organization culture as

> a pattern of shared basic assumptions that the group learned as it solved its problems of external adaptation and internal integration, that has worked well enough to be considered valid and, therefore, to be taught to new members as the correct way you perceive, think, and feel in relation to those problems.[2]

Some of the critical components of organizational culture include regular communication patterns, norms shared and valued by employees, top management's attitude and behavior toward policymaking and implementation, and general climate of the organization.

Development of a CRM-inclusive business culture will require that the employees, as well as the managers, are aware of expectations and responsibilities. Making CRM an integral part of a company's strategy will require contributions from every individual, and one of the ways to enforce contribution is to increase accountability for each concerned person. Making individuals accountable has a positive influence on their involvement in a CRM initiative. However, the success of this approach depends entirely on whether the new roles these individuals are expected to fill have been clearly communicated or not. It should not be a surprise if some employees resist this change. Therefore, top management should be ready with a clear action plan to deal with such situations as they emerge. Top management also needs to assess the status of three critical aspects of the organizational culture—communication, collaboration, and learning—in order to make an informative decision regarding CRM selection. The following is a detailed discussion on these three aspects:

1. Communication. To assimilate CRM into the philosophy of an organization, communication links among employees, as well as departments, need to be in place and working. Organizations can use technology to build these links; however, sharing of information is possible only if individuals are willing to participate. The best way to realize this dream is the development of an organizational culture that fosters the communication of information. Yet, building such an environment will have its challenges.

Supervisors who successfully experiment and develop innovative methods for the collection and dissemination of CRM intelligence should be applauded and given incentives. Customer-facing employees, such as salespeople, bring the intelligence from the market and feed it into the CRM system, and they should be rewarded, too. In organizations where the sharing of thoughts and information is praised, employees will be motivated to demonstrate behaviors beyond their job requirements related to problem solving, teamwork, knowledge discovery, social networking within the organization, and relationship building with colleagues. Notably, these behaviors are critical for the success of a CRM initiative in any organization, and they should be both valued and encouraged.

Without doubt, information sharing yields positive results for a company; however, it is a rare occurrence when management publicizes such instances. In general, an individual employee, manager, or department claims all the credit for the creation of an organizational culture that promotes communication among departments and individuals.

Organizations must highlight the positive outcomes of information-sharing initiatives so that other members will be motivated to follow such a path.

2. Collaboration. Often, CRM is perceived as a tool or technology dedicated to helping the marketing, sales, and customer service divisions. This incorrect perception hinders collaboration efforts within an organization and should not be ignored. Top management should do their best to make sure that the CRM initiative receives support from each department. After all, customer satisfaction is the lifeline for any business, and every functional unit should understand that. Collaboration will create a professional network within the organization where leaders and employees are not forced to think and act solely in linear fashion.

For CRM initiatives to be successful, employees and departments will need to perform as integrated teams instead of individuals or detached functional units. Unlike other software systems that are designed specifically for one business function, such as accounting or operation management, a CRM solution has organization-wide scope, so all of the departments and employees across the company use it. When deployed in an organization, CRM solutions aggregate vast amounts of information to create a pool of knowledge that can be used to prospect new business, validate leads, analyze processes, and more. Department leaders and supervisors should meet on a regular basis to discuss ideas and strategies for improving customer satisfaction and loyalty. Collaboration is essential in developing an organizational culture that is conducive to CRM. In general, different business units in any organization aim to achieve their unique and department specific goals, and this often creates isolation. This philosophy of isolation creates a vacuum, and one entity that typically suffers is the customer. In some cases, organizations face intense rivalry and unhealthy competition between their own functional units, causing the situation to worsen. Such problems need to be addressed and resolved in order to create a supportive CRM culture.

A CRM strategy takes into consideration a way of thinking, interacting, and collaborating with others in the organization. The success of CRM as a solution and strategy depends on the realization of a collaborative working environment, one that is free of isolation. As a common practice in many organizations, individuals are skeptical of sharing information or collaborating on a project for fear of losing individual gains. To overcome skepticism, it is essential for an organization's leaders to inject a collaborative mentality into the work culture and display the deployment of CRM technology as an opportunity for all to collaborate and work together.

3. Learning. Organizations and individuals alike are faced with a wealth of information as technology innovations occur on a daily basis, making use of technology as easy as it can be. With a large inflow of information, organizations find it difficult to retain and manage this information. Considering information as an input to the knowledge creation process, proper knowledge management is becoming increasingly difficult. For this reason, many organizations are developing and modifying their learning philosophies. For an organization to adapt a cultural change, learning must take place. In the context of CRM, the organization learning will occur among employees, management, and customers. Knowledge management, in this case, will include collecting, storing, managing, analyzing, and disseminating customer knowledge throughout the organization.

In order to adapt and implement a CRM strategy, firms need to have, or develop, an ability to learn. Within an organization, individuals need to understand what knowledge they need to gain, how they should maintain such knowledge, where they can find the information that will lead to knowledge, and how they can use this knowledge effectively. Considering that learning starts with collecting information, a firm has to assess its ability to conduct high-quality interactions with customers, which can further lead to increased information exchange. Firm-customer interactions may occur across several different channels, and a plan for managing the inflow of information from all customer touch points needs to be in place. It is important to keep in mind that individual learning and organizational learning are complementary to each other, and any cultural change involving learning should include individual employees. Learning and cultural transformation will require a change in attitudes and behaviors at all levels. To support and motivate learning at an individual level, the organization may need to change their compensation system, reinforcing new behaviors.

For CRM success, it is essential to have a mechanism for coordination that enables an organization to identify with its customers through collaborating with them and responding to their needs. In a situation where a firm lacks such abilities, the CRM initiative will face tough resistance from within organization. Selection of a specific CRM software that is most compatible with the organization's capabilities to learn and adapt will help in reducing employee resistance. Therefore, the decision should take into consideration the company fit; employee fit; user support, needs, and requirements; and the organization's ability as a whole to adapt a change. The development of a culture in which the organization focuses on learning can eventually enable the firm to leverage organization-wide intellectual property such as operational know-how, customer service discoveries, original customer data, and creative methods that would otherwise remain unnoticed. With a learning environment in place, an organization will be better able to widen its customer base, optimize productivity, and increase profitability.

Customer-Centric Environment

The primary feature of a customer-centric environment is that all business activities are geared toward customers. The most prominent outcome of a successful CRM system is enhanced and positive customer service. Thus, a good CRM system and customer-centric environment will prove complementary to each other. Identification of profitable customers was once the most challenging task for an organization; however, CRM programs have made this task easier and more achievable. Establishment and management of interactive relationships with profitable customers can be materialized with the help of a CRM system.

A company should focus primarily on customers because without them there is no business in the first place. A true customer-centric organization is one that is capable of employing technology productively, using customer information competently, and maintaining a high-quality customer service workforce. Investment in CRM technology will not produce desired outcomes unless the organization develops a customer-centric environment. At the broader level, a customer-centric organization will stand on three pillars, which are discussed below.

1. Customer-Centric Technology. It will be nearly impossible to sustain a customer-centric approach without the appropriate technology to support it. Customers are now empowered through several technological innovations, but that does not mean that they will automatically start talking to the organization about their concerns. It is up to companies to encourage customers to interact with them and to provide them with easy channels for interactions. This cannot be done without the proper technology and tools. In order to bring customers in to the communication chain, organizations need to ensure customers that their voices will be heard and their concerns will be addressed in a timely fashion. Technology tools will be necessary in drawing and accessing a comprehensive view of a customer, which will be the stepping-stone for building a customer-focused organization. Even a wealth of information will not be of value to the company unless useful insights can be drawn from the data. Sophisticated tools and techniques are required for analyzing customer-related matrices such as customer expectations, customer satisfaction, purchase intentions, and so on.

2. Customer-Centric Workforce. Another key element that is needed for building a customer-centric organization is the effectiveness of the employees serving the customers. CRM will be beneficial only in the case where an organization's workforce, especially customer-facing employees, is committed to producing value for customers. Customer contact should not be considered data collection; instead, the focus should be on providing customers with value and positive experiences. Development of a customer-centric workforce requires a shift in employee thinking and focus from a transactional approach to a relational approach. A customer-centric culture should nurture a business plan seeking to fulfill customer needs instead of operational needs and to promote customer orientation instead of product orientation. In organizations characterized by an internal environment where employees do not worry about positive customer experiences, CRM would not do any good. Having a customer-centric workforce is the key to CRM success and is an invaluable tool for the pursuit of better customer relationships.

3. Customer-Centric Processes. Today's customers enjoy the luxury of choosing a vendor from an array of companies. Being aware of the fact that the product itself is no longer the sole criterion for differentiation among manufacturers, consumers seek overall value they receive for money they pay. This includes a quick and reliable delivery system, availability of different payment options, multiple yet active communication channels, and so on. A customer might derive the value of an exchange process with an organization from several sources. Therefore, it is necessary to instill customer focus into all organizational processes, including solution development, customer learning, knowledge transfer, decision making, actual purchases, solution implementation, and management and repair.

There is no one magic solution for fixing customer service or for making a company customer-centric. It is a long-term process, and, more than anything, the process requires innovative ideas specific to the company and industry that will help create a customer-focused environment. Just as organizations consider product innovation crucial to their survival, they should also adopt the philosophy that customer service is crucial to survival as well. Making customers their center of attention will help organizations to reap financial rewards. More and more, firms are beginning to understand the importance of customer relationships, and they desire establishing strong relationships with their customers. These firms, however, must understand that relationships are built through the groundwork of positive customer experiences, and a few bad experiences can jeopardize the company-customer bond. Organizations should seek to build customer experiences related to their products and services at several levels, including top management, the finance and accounting divisions, the information technology department, and so on. It is important to recognize that such experience-building efforts will require the participation of all the members of the value chain, including suppliers, retailers, distributors, and the like.

Top Management Commitment

Top management's commitment to the adaptation and implementation of CRM technology is one of the most critical issues in adopting this technology. In order to understand the reasons why commitment is so important, we need to address the question of why CRM and conventional organizational cultures experience difficulty in "getting along." Unfortunately, very few corporations really care about customers as they try to create "customer value" and enhance "customer experience." Most organizations still adopt the traditional monetary "profit-loss" approach. For such organizations and their leaders, it is difficult to make a big investment that yields intangible returns such as shaping a better "customer experience." This demonstrates their inability in seeing the return on investment (ROI) over the long term. In addition, "CRM" is still a mystery term to many executives, and they often confuse it with other tools and techniques such as data warehousing, enterprise resource planning, and the like. The truth is that CRM is much more than a database or a centralized software system.

The success of CRM implementation requires complete and unwavering support from top management, which needs to supervise the appropriate organizational changes and demonstrate a long-term commitment to the CRM project. Moreover, management needs to communicate this commitment and its vision to its immediate subordinates and other employees throughout the organization. Considering the cost, sources of funding need to be recognized and secured by top executives. Empowering leadership behaviors such as participation in decision making, removal of bureaucratic constraints, and meaningfulness of work can also help in developing a positive and smooth employee transition from an old to new cultural environment.

Overall, company leaders need to have a vision that considers customers as the top priority. This vision should be reflected in the actions of top management on a routine basis. In order to place CRM strategy at the center of business operations, leadership needs to demonstrate its commitment to it. If CRM takes a backseat and is turned into a tool that teams use as they please, gaining an ROI on CRM will become an uphill battle. When top management makes a mindful decision to promote, support, and engage in actions that set the tone for others in the company, change management takes on its best form. Fundamental changes within an organization take time, and, during the transition phase, senior managers should act as role models and teachers. These leaders become champions for the change or technology that is forthcoming. As leaders in the change, it is very possible that they will be the deciding factor in success or failure.

External Assessment

It can be argued that CRM software is on its way to becoming a commodity, and the only way to stop this is to establish this technology solution as a strategy, not just as an application that does sophisticated record keeping. Every day, new companies pop up and claim to offer a solution for CRM. The term "CRM" is being used very loosely, and there needs to be some checks and balances in place to establish a sense of responsibility. How to serve customers effectively requires different solutions for different organizations; therefore, every company should have a customized strategy and identify key points before selecting a CRM solution.

As a cautionary note, firms should select a CRM vendor that has an established presence in the market and that can expand the solution if the company's needs change in the future. At a minimum, a CRM solution should have some basic attributes, such as a flexible and powerful application platform, customization abilities, robust analytical capabilities, and low total cost of ownership. In terms of advanced functionality, there are some applications that may be useful for companies operating in a globally competitive world, such as geographic customer-base management, competitive intelligence, content management, advanced analytics, and workflow design. Selection of a vendor should also take in to consideration the availability of an experienced and dedicated consulting staff. Expert team members from the supplier's company are the key to ensuring success.

In the case of industry-specific solutions, it would be wise to find out about a vendor's reputation in the market by talking to other users in the industry. Choosing an accurate variety of functionality means that the choice meets the firm's business needs but does not go overboard in capturing every possible function. CRM packages offer numerous features to serve immensely different business environments. Therefore, it is very important to focus on each company's specific needs. For example, the majority of CRM applications offer out-of-the-box pricing modules that are usually based on the quantity or unit price model. Considering each company's own discount policies and strategies, it would be difficult to develop a standard module that fits all.

Vendors keep on adding features to their CRM packages in order to remain competitive in an intense market. For example, some CRM applications offer scripting for the selling process. As sales organizations migrate from closed-box selling to an adaptive selling approach, having a script might create a dilemma for salespeople rather than helping them. Finally, if a particular functionality is critical for one company, it does not mean it will be helpful for every company, even within the same industry.

A CRM system should be able to integrate back-office applications and other business systems, and it should be accessible from any setting, including remote locations. Even if the company does not have a global presence, it would not hurt to have a global perspective when shopping for a CRM application. Companies that are global should be aware of some key points, such as whether the vendor is able to provide support at international locations, whether software is simultaneously available in other languages, and whether the software offers multiple currency support.

Case 4. CRM Selection at ABN AMRO Asset Management

ABN AMRO Asset Management (AAAM) is the independent division of ABN AMRO bank, with assets of $205 billion under management. Some of the prominent clients among its 2,000 institutional customers include central banks, insurance firms, and pension funds. However, with the company's growth, some unique problems were originating. Because AAAM operates in 22 countries, each office had a different working style, a different time zone, a different system for storing customer interactions, and so on. Management was facing difficulties in measuring precise sales performance as well as keeping track of other information such as customer profitability and time allocation.

The executive management soon realized that they needed a CRM system in order to have the ability to view their global customer base from a single window. The company hired Accenture, a prominent player in the field of consulting and outsourcing, to outline an action plan that would support a better organized and performance-measured sales process.

After constructing a framework for the sales process, Accenture started examining potential solutions within the firm's project guidelines. A customized demonstration followed the examination, and Accenture finally recommended that AAAM deploy a Microsoft CRM solution. Accenture outlined some primary reasons for this selection:

1. Microsoft CRM was easy to implement and very user-friendly. For AAAM, it meant that its salespeople

would adopt this technology easily and quickly when compared to other applications. This would fulfill the company's objective of implementing the system in a fast manner. Because of implementing a less complex system, training could be easy and short.

2. AAAM wanted to have a long-lasting relationship with the CRM vendor. Management was aware of the availability of numerous short-performing CRM vendors in the market place, so they wanted a partner who could grow with them. With Microsoft, the company was assured that the solution would be supported throughout its life cycle.

To avoid any risks related to the implementation of the CRM technology, AAAM picked Avanade as a partner in the implementation project. Avanade, a global services company exclusively focused on Microsoft technology, brought extensive CRM experience, ensuring a good fit between the CRM solution and AAAM's existing infrastructure. Avanade began its implementation by taking data from AAAM's financial system, including customer contact details, contact and account history, and product information, and started feeding this data into the CRM-based solution. The goal was to enable users to enter new data directly into the new system as well as to access relevant customer information in real time with absolute ease. In order to have one accurate report, the salespeople's e-mails, planning calendars, and notes were synchronized. This effort not only helped management to keep track of their sales team but also helped salespeople to improve responsiveness and customer service.

Source: Microsoft Dynamics (2005, September).

CHAPTER 5

System Planning and Designing

Careful planning is required before an organization actually starts implementing a customer relationship management (CRM) system, and the most important principle is to keep the process simple. Organizations often get into the mode of reinventing the wheel while incorporating the CRM system into its existing structure. Only in rare occasions is it necessary for organizations to reconstruct the whole system from scratch. The focus should be on capitalizing on the resources and processes that the organization already has in place. This will flatten the learning curve for the workforce. Yet, there will be some areas where firms do need to start fresh, and such decisions should not be taken lightly. Planning and patience are required while designing and reconstructing the system so that CRM technology can fit in well. The most critical step is to clearly understand the current business approach and to assess the infrastructure that supports this approach.

Generic Versus Customized Solution

People often confuse direct selling with customized one-to-one selling even though these two approaches are inherently different. Direct selling is an approach where an organization has decided to aim marketing communication directly at consumers in an attempt to sell products and services to them without using intermediaries. In this context, however, it may be the case that the organization is selling a generic product to all customers. On the other hand, a customization approach is not about selling directly to individual customers but is instead about solving individual customer needs by providing them with customized solutions. CRM is all about one-to-one customer relationships. It enables organizations to treat each customer differently. For example, a pioneer of the responsive supply chain, Dell Inc. deals with customers individually and offers customized products. Nevertheless, for them, it is not direct selling that is important but one-to-one marketing and satisfying one customer at a time.

Customization is only possible if an organization's database contains specific details about customer needs and wants. CRM technology enables businesses to offer customized products and services. Here, collection of information takes a different approach, where firms collect market knowledge through rich interactions with customers, keeping in mind that their success is not in getting more customers but in retaining and growing with them. The real power of one-to-one business practices emerges from the "learning relationship." It is a process where a firm interacts with the customer, and based on what they have learned about the customer, the firm tailors their product or service or elements associated with it. In essence, what the firm really tries to do is to give the customer a reason to invest time and effort in teaching the firm how to serve his or her business.

The more time customers invest in building relationship with an organization, the more the stake they have in making this relationship work. For example, a company willing to improve customer service through technology enhancements hires a technology provider. Now, if the company is investing in terms of money and time by setting up a buying center and a team of trainees, they want the seller to succeed. In the event of failure, the buyer has to go to another company and repeat the whole process. The more time buyers invest in telling a seller what they need and how to serve their business, the more they have at stake. Organizational buyers especially do not want to reinvent the relationship. Hence, if a company desires customer loyalty, they should demonstrate this feeling to the customer. Responding to the call, the buyer would generally take the time to teach the seller how to better serve his or her business. In return, based on this feedback from the buyer, the seller should change the treatment such as service and support offerings because this adaptability and responsiveness is the essence of the learning relationship.

CRM enables organizations to execute two basic processes of one-to-one marketing: customer interaction and product customization (Figure 5.1). With a sophisticated CRM system in place, a firm can demonstrate that

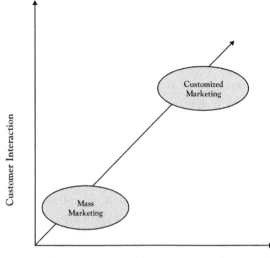

Figure 5.1. *An organization's marketing approach and CRM dimensions.*

it remembers specific customers when they come back and can make the buying process easier for them. It also helps reduce overall cost in the long run by lowering operating expenses (no need to relearn about the customer every time they approach the firm) and also reducing inventory costs. There are definite reasons to believe that knowing the customers will help improve profits for a company. With sound knowledge about its customer base, a firm can concentrate on the best customers and can customize its products and services as per their needs, treat the middle range, where customers are not currently giving a lot of profit to a company but they have the potential to do so, as a significant group, which requires moderate customization, and discourage bottom-feeders, or customers who are not contributing to the overall profit in any significant way and their future prospects of doing so are also weak.

Infrastructure

As previously mentioned, CRM is not just a product, service, technology tool, or software; rather, it is a business strategy. Therefore, an appropriate combination of humans and technology is needed to build a CRM infrastructure. It is often the case that organizations who want to build a customer-focused technology infrastructure simply replace their traditional customer-interaction technology system, which contains a voice-only call center or an Internet-only electronic service, with multichannel customer-interaction systems combining web, telecommunication, and field sales channels. In doing so, the human part of the infrastructure is ignored. For example, an unprepared and overpersuasive telemarketer who calls a customer without knowing that the customer's family is actually enjoying their culture- or religion-specific holiday at that time can actually upset the relationship.

CRM should be viewed as a continuous process, and the key to success will be to have an infrastructure made up of humans and technology that facilitates this process. Customer data collection capabilities and data storage availability are the initiating factors, while the tools, techniques, and expertise to develop and manage information will form another critical requirement. Systems and processes that enable a firm to create value (i.e., collaborative solutions, customized products, relevant promotions) and enrich customer service (effective call center, complaints resolutions, automated sales process, etc.) are necessary to keep this process running and should be considered fundamental parts of this infrastructure as well (Figure 5.2). CRM technology will facilitate this process by creating visibility across all channels such as the company website, call center, field sales force, retailers, and partners that, in turn, will drive better service delivery across all business units. These customer contact units will feed CRM systems with customer information and, at the same time, will receive critical customer information from the CRM system that will help to serve customers better.

Still, there are some other important points that should be considered when building a CRM infrastructure. For example, the organization should bridge front- and back-office systems to incorporate records of customer contact, product information requests, purchases, and service requests. In addition, customers should be allowed to interact with the firm through any touch point they desire, including the web, phone, and personal meetings.

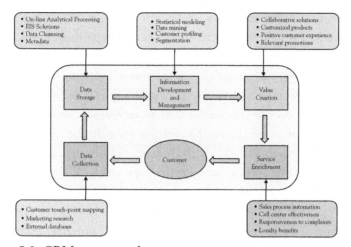

Figure 5.2. CRM *process and components.*

Reengineering of Structures, Systems, and Processes

Given rapid technology innovations and intense competition in the marketplace, companies try to keep themselves up-to-date in terms of the latest technology tools and techniques. CRM implementation, however, will require some reengineering of already-present structures, systems, and processes. The key here is to use available tools from a CRM perspective. Systems should be set and processes should be executed with rich customer experiences being the ultimate goal. This restructuring should be done in such a way that the following factors are addressed:

- Customers have multiple points of access.
- Customers have options and the ability to perform self-service.
- Customers receive customized solutions and services.
- Speed of order delivery and after-sales service are fast.

A company's electronic business solutions should offer value propositions by integrating with the business processes of partners and customers. The system should also be set up in such a way that the company is able to extend its business applications to organizational clients and tailor products and services to the end users' needs. From a CRM perspective, a company's website should be used as a medium for customers to access accounts and make inquiries as per their convenience around the clock. The process of electronic bill access and payment is widely used among organizations, but it is the user friendliness it provides that makes a customer feel empowered. Some customers, especially senior citizens, are not comfortable with web technology and prefer to interact with the organization over the phone. To cater to such needs, an effective interactive voice response system should be in place. In the case of live customer service over the phone, the firm should integrate intelligent call routing with available call center technology such as Voice over Internet Protocol (VoIP) or private branch exchange (PBX). This integration will help maintain the efficiency of the call center and reduce the number of dropped calls, which are big concerns from a customer perspective. These efforts will be greatly supported by the availability of an integrated technology framework that interfaces different applications and databases containing customer information. Finally, reliable reporting tools will be required for internal as well as external purposes.

Complete Involvement

In today's market-oriented and highly competitive market, it is hard to imagine any unit or department of a company that is not somehow related to customer value offerings. For example, some units produce products for customers, some sell products to customers, and some handle financial transactions with customers. Considering that most of the functions within an organization are centered on the customer, it is essential to include all of them in the deployment of a CRM system. Complete involvement is not an option anymore—it is a requirement.

The fact is that software represents only one part of any CRM initiative. CRM vendors provide organizations with tools, and sometimes even staff, to guide and manage the implementation process; however, it is the combination of people, process, and technology that is needed to realize successful implementation. Depending on the type of CRM solution and services offered by vendors, a CRM project might require more or less system administration and management. However, the concerned organization and its employees have to accept ownership for the deployment and operations to be productive. The company may create a supervisory leadership or steering committee to act as the central unit for the project, thereby offering the much-needed visibility and account-ability for the task's success. The formation of a cross-functional team of representatives—those who are knowledgeable of the business' processes and requirements—is another critical step.

A good option for some organizations is to recruit a third party that specializes in implementation and execution of CRM solutions. Several companies offer such services and bring experience and innovation to each phase of the CRM project. Specifically, services may include CRM suite deployment, system integration, executive dashboards for analysis services, enterprise portals for content management, collaborative work platforms, and business process management.

Case 5. CRM Planning and Implementation at 3M

Big firms that carry diverse product portfolios may find CRM technology as a critical resource for providing good customer service. However, in such cases, a stepwise approach toward CRM implementation is the most pragmatic one. The case of 3M's CRM solution initiative offers several possibilities for such a course of action. 3M is a diversified company with global sales of $25 billion (fiscal year 2008), a 79,000-strong workforce, and operations in over 60 countries. The company sustains diversity in product offerings by applying technologies across a wide array of customer needs.

Witnessing an increasingly complex product portfolio, 3M's call center unit was finding it difficult to respond satisfactorily to customer queries. To address the problem, the company decided to implement CRM and knowledge management (KM) technologies. After detailed analysis of their call-center operations, they carved out key objectives that needed to be achieved through a CRM system. Some of the goals included improvement in accuracy of solutions offered to customers and in the speed of problem resolution. The company decided to take a strategic path leading to successful implementation.

The first step was to explore available technology options. For this purpose, a 14-member team was created and assigned to this task. In order to bring different perspectives to the table, the task force included call center agents, customer service managers, information technology managers, and documentation developers. Next, the task force assessed multiple options available in the marketplace and recommended one software solution that was easy to integrate with other KM solution products and that required the least amount of programming prior to implementation.

The company management carefully watched the performance of this system over time and eventually declared it as a success. Once the goals were achieved at the level of the call center, the company decided to implement the software in other departments, beginning with the human relations and purchasing units. The goal of this was to empower these units so that they could answer questions coming from business partners as well as other employees.

Finally, a central knowledge base was made available via the company intranet. The goal was to make information accessible for all employees within the organization.

Source: ICFAI Center for Management Research (2002).

CHAPTER 6

Implementation of Designed Systems

Once a project budget is approved, most organizations want to implement their customer relationship management (CRM) system quickly. Implementation of CRM, however, does not happen overnight and is tactical and methodical in nature. Yet, while firms can speed up the process of software implementation, CRM adoption as a cultural transition is difficult to accelerate. Investment, even in the best technology, is of no worth unless employees feel comfortable with it. In order for users to be comfortable, patience and planning will be required from management and support, and training from the vendor will be required. It is recommended that companies consider the services of CRM experts working for the vendor, as they can be great consultants, especially since they are the ones who developed the specific software product—they might be the best source of knowledge and guidance in making the most of that CRM solution. Intense competition in the CRM market has also prompted vendors to offer value-added services to their customers, and helping the customer implement the system is definitely one of them. Still, the implementation process will take meticulous and consistent efforts from the organization side of the equation.

CRM implementation should not be seen, in any way, as a stand-alone process that is confined within the boundaries of the marketing department or information technology (IT) department. Instead, the implementation of CRM should be synchronized with other processes inside, as well as outside, specific departments. Expectations should be pragmatic, and appropriate resources should be provided. Top management should execute this implementation process with the utmost importance, and implementation should take place in small phases. It would be unreasonable to expect CRM to improve results within the organization if work conditions remain unchanged. Even if the management has carved out the customer strategy and product strategy, a well-designed strategy for implementation will be required for the success of the CRM initiative. There are several issues that need to be addressed and several steps that need to be taken in order to have successful CRM implementation.

Training

To ensure success in any technological project, it is necessary to provide users, as well as other project participants, with the proper training and education. If the parties related to the project do not have a clear understanding of the expectations related to system functionality, the system will either be underused or users' expectations will be too high to be realized. The good news is that all major software vendors understand the value of user buy-in when providing a new technology or application, and a CRM project is no different. In order to offer a better perspective regarding training, we address two key questions: why should organizations need to consider it necessary, and how exactly should training take place?

Why Is It Necessary?

Employees in any given organization perform very different tasks, and their approach may not include the strategic use of technology or, in some cases, even a basic use of technology. Yet, for the utilization of CRM technology, users need to have general IT skill, and, moreover, they should have knowledge of the technical and organizational concepts of CRM. A deficiency of technical skills fuels insecurity and uncertainty among employees, and, consequently, they may resist the change. In another context, users may have the required technical skills but lack the business understanding of CRM, which also is essential for its strategic use.

Time and again, the need for a systematic training program does not receive proper attention, and, unfortunately, users are left without a comprehensive understanding of the system. It has been argued that one of the reasons why CRM systems often do not produce expected results is because users use less than half of the functions offered by its applications.

With that said, the primary reasons cited for taking a shortcut in training are the lack of recourses, such as skills and finances, and the lack of time because of delays in the implementation schedule.

How Should It Be Done?

It is important to conduct an extensive CRM training program for employees. Training programs should highlight the importance of CRM in the current market context and also the benefits for employees if they participate in the CRM implementation. The focus should not be on how to become a technology expert; instead, training should cover a wide range of issues related to CRM. For example, training should provide users early assistance in terms of software implementation and use, report generation, and information management. It is important for management to review and understand available technical baselines before setting goals for any training program.

Employees should be trained in the basics of CRM, such as its operational structure, applications, what it covers, and where it came from. Employees should also be aware of the fact that CRM use is no longer just an option that they can choose to ignore; instead, it is a basic necessity for organizations to survive, and their own survival depends on it. Consequences for not using CRM should be a topic of discussion with employees and managers. A sudden and steep learning curve could push away some employees and managers from practicing CRM, and the only way to resolve this problem is to consistently employ these tools and techniques.

For organizations, it is not a brilliant idea to give all the training related responsibilities to their own IT unit members. Technical vocabulary is inherently different from business vocabulary, and mixing them together can create some serious problems. Empowering future users will motivate them to learn and explore the system. People who can speak their language should guide them in this process. Thus, some vendors provide training as part of the software purchase, and it often proves fruitful. In the case that training is not included, it will be worthwhile to add it to the purchase.

Support Within the Organization

The decision to implement CRM needs to be viewed as an organization-wide change; therefore, if the change is to be successful, support must come from each section of the company. The key is to get everybody involved because all units are directly or indirectly dealing with customers, and each unit may have knowledge about customers that can be leveraged. Generally, customer-facing units, such as sales, marketing, and call centers, are champions of CRM initiatives and early supporters of the initiative. However, management should make an effort to integrate all of the units and employees.

The first step in this process should be securing top management sponsorship in the CRM project. Without having a clear vision, mission, and commitment from top management, the future of the CRM initiative is in jeopardy. After securing top management's support, the next target should be actual users of the system. All of the critical variables—such as training, communication, motivation, support, and recognition—that can influence the outcome of the CRM initiative should be taken into consideration. Bringing CRM into the organization will affect, directly or indirectly, every department of the company, and the heads of all divisions should support the project. Their willingness to support this change will be necessary in creating an overall welcoming environment.

A CRM project team should consist of hardworking people who have the ability to be diligent and understand how the information silos within an organization can, and should, be integrated. Notably, finding key issues related to people and highlighting them as part of the overall objective can be a good way to widen support within the organization. Employees who are best known for their knowledge and expertise of the organization's business processes can play key roles in defining the processes to CRM technicians. Employees taking an active part in the implementation will help in developing the basic and essential requirements of the business that will eventually help integrate the CRM with the existing business system. Moreover, being "part of the family" will allow them to be the advocates for CRM and, in general, the change initiative.

Project Management

CRM deployment is a long and complex project and thus needs coordinated efforts, a well-defined schedule, and unbiased monitoring of checkpoints. A CRM system supports a new way of thinking and a different approach toward actions in comparison to old business practices. Therefore, unlike other project management tasks, managing the changed initiative is crucial in CRM project management.

First, primary responsibilities should be divided in two higher level segments: strategic responsibilities and operational responsibilities. Strategic responsibilities involve the transition from the old to the new culture; coordination with other projects, both within the focal organization and between organizations within the supply chain; maintaining communication with the CRM supplier as well as involvement of the CRM supplier; and keeping top management in the loop so that the project remains viable for them. On the contrary, operational responsibilities include development of interfaces, quality and security of data transferring, and managing the execution of processes.

Good initiation of a project is critical, but it alone will not guarantee the success of the project; hence, continuous efforts will be needed for the project to be successful. There are always different kinds of hurdles associated with a project that can cause delays, so it will be helpful if project managers meticulously follow the progress of the project. Finally, it can also be helpful to have an alternate plan in case something unexpected happens so that implementation is not completely halted.

CRM Data Security

During and after the CRM implementation process, it is highly recommended that organizations look into their CRM data security environment and scrutinize each spot that has even a distant possibility of a security breach. Inherently, CRM applications offer data mobility, and it is considered as a great benefit; however, it also makes data vulnerable to falling into the wrong hands. To avoid such instances, remote data should be encrypted. At a very basic level, all mobile devices should be protected. Special vigilance is required when transferring data from one location to another. Some promote the use of virtual private networks (VPNs) when accessing data. VPNs function as personal links between an organization's remote system and the public network server, and they offer data encryption at both sender and receiver locations.

Lack of alertness by employees is one of the main causes for data mishandling and security breaches. Companies should deal with this issue seriously and should have a clear plan for maintaining the security of their data. Employees should be given training on data security and should be encouraged to follow basic safety measures in their day-to-day operations. In addition, users should be made accountable for data security. Management should keep track of employees who are given data access privileges and motivate them to act as safety guards.

Implementation Steps

The implementation of CRM technology is a complex task requiring a systematic approach. The following significant steps summarize the implementation process:

- *Matching issues and opportunities.* The CRM implementation process should begin by identifying core business issues and charting the opportunities presented by CRM technology in addressing those issues. Implementation of CRM should be viewed as an opportunity to review work procedures across the organization. To begin with, the management team and the implementation team should analyze and evaluate business processes and data sources that are to be integrated into the CRM system.

- *Finding a middle path.* Sometimes it is not pragmatic to address all the issues concerning different departments at one time. Each business unit has its own objectives and priorities, and they each may have their own ways of achieving these goals and objectives. Similarly, a CRM implementation project can have different meanings for different business units. For example, the IT division may seek an uneventful implementation and unwavering uptime. On the other hand, the priority of sales and marketing leaders would be to report attributes and abilities required to customize the system. It is advisable to identify similarities and differences among various business issues and prioritize them based on immediate firm requirements. In order to find a middle path, CRM project managers should initiate early dialogs with all the users and work accordingly so that the best-suited system can be implemented without compromising quality.

- *Segmenting the project.* This stage is all about project planning and methodology. The organization may want to break down their CRM project into controllable parts by designing a pilot program and short-range milestones. For example, an organization with global trade operations may arrange the CRM implementation project by country or location. Some organizations do it by departments or by strategic business units. Launching a series of small and controllable projects is far more pragmatic than going all out for the deployment of one vast all-encompassing project. A segmented implementation approach provides flexibility to the firm as well as to the CRM project team so that they can make alterations and handle expectations at a reasonable level.

- *Demonstrating success.* To keep things moving and to maintain credibility, it will be helpful to demonstrate some quick results. A pilot project involving relevant business units and employees that is small enough to allow modifications during the course of the project, and big enough to get things rolling, can be extremely helpful in the overall schema. In addition, this approach can help a firm satisfy each department's needs and thereby ensure that the technology solution becomes an operational part of their regular functions. A good strategy for managers would be to highlight the success and promote the benefits garnered by the company as a result of those achievements.

- *Planning conservatively.* During CRM implementation, conservative planning should be practiced, and adventures should be avoided as much as possible. Those who are involved in the implementation project should convey the harsh realities to the other members in the organization and should not attempt to sugarcoat the process in any way. On the technological front, it is advisable to develop a considerable multiyear technical architecture plan. Vigilance is required while collecting and storing the data, as acquiring and storing useless data wastes effort, time, and money. Successful implementation will require several rounds of data collection within the organization. Nevertheless, it is critical not to underestimate how much information will get the job done because later on, depending on the circumstances, the organization should be ready to expand the system.

- *Respecting customer's information.* The customer is the focal point of a CRM system. Therefore, during the pilot project, or at any stage, the organization must recognize and respect the customer's individuality and privacy. The majority of data-related security breaches can be linked back to internal business sources such as faulty processes and careless or untrained employees. Apart from this, CRM suppliers could also make a mistake that would be harmful for the company, as customers will be concerned with the company not the supplier. Therefore, security practices of the vendor, as well as the company, need to be carefully monitored.

- *Keeping top management in the loop.* For successful implementation, obtaining and maintaining the support from top management is essential. In reality, a CRM initiative starts and concludes at the top management level of an organization. It is not possible for organizations to have success with a CRM project without a complete management buy-in. On the same note, top management cannot just walk away from the project after initiating it. In order to keep top management in the loop, the project team should constantly provide leaders and decision makers with their CRM program observations and recommendations as they emerge. A good way to keep track of all the events is to prepare the CRM implementation business case.

Define Objectives and Analyze Performance

Considering the significant amount of investment in terms of time, effort, and money, organizations look for a sufficient return on investment (ROI) on their CRM project so that they can justify the investment. An organization that keeps taking actions to develop relationships but does not measure the outcomes will neither receive a return on their investment nor gain any customer knowledge. Similarly, investment in technology without recognition of its role in relationship building will cost the company a fortune. It is important to mention, however, that the success of CRM implementation should not be limited to only the sales department or salespeople but should also include customer support employees, billing and accounts receivable functions, public relations, advertising, and so on.

Monitoring the performance of the CRM system is a part of the CRM implementation process. Firms need to track key metrics such as the optimization of the sales cycle, patterns of sales increases or decreases, cost-effectiveness, profitability, and customer satisfaction in order to answer how well CRM has delivered results and served the company's business purposes. Research in this context suggests that a sophisticated CRM system generally helps an organization to increase revenue by 10%–20% and customer retention by 10%. Such increases may provide strong justification for the implementation of a CRM system.

CRM is all about the customer, and, therefore, organizations need to make sure that they analyze the performance metrics related to the customer's point of view. Organizations should keep in mind that the basic purpose of implementing CRM is to serve customers in a better way and to leverage marketing plans and strategies based on customer value and requirements. Successful CRM system implementation should provide the organization with flexibility related to product customization, pricing, customer service, and the like. Therefore, the best way to evaluate the CRM system's performance is to determine customer desires and then determine how the CRM system is contributing in fulfilling those needs and desires. CRM strategy contains both business and technology perspectives. Once objectives are clearly defined, the organization needs to analyze performance at several levels. Recent research[1] in this area proposes multiple performance indicators for CRM (see Figure 6.1).

Performance objectives should be defined from both a business and a technology perspective. If an organization is tracking only financial measures, it will not capture the real performance of the CRM system. There is no doubt that financial measures provide an objective and quantifiable assessment; however, such measures do not say much about customer outcomes, which are the essence of any CRM strategy. In order to outline a unified and comprehensive approach for long-term competitive success, performance measures should reflect several key perspectives, such as monetary objectives, customer performance, and internal business processes and the infrastructure to support them.

Successful CRM implementation means a firm is able to get a comprehensive view of its customers. CRM technology provides valuable inputs to an organization's marketing research efforts. This implementation can also facilitate the analysis of customers, their buying patterns, and their reasons for decision making, or, "to buy or not to buy." For example, identifying customers who are susceptible to up-selling or cross-selling opportunities provides firms with the ability to recognize the

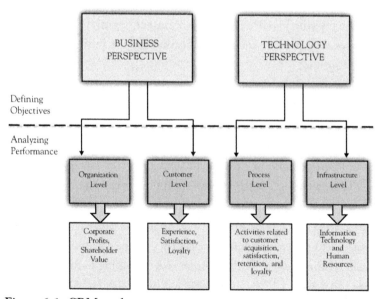

Figure 6.1. CRM *performance measurement.*

characteristics of such customers so that they can locate customers with same characteristics in the future. Notably, such efforts can be fruitful only if every customer-contact unit is well integrated and coordinated. In addition, the evaluation of results should be done in such a way that it facilitates continuous learning within the organization. Without learning, it will be impossible for the organization to realize the CRM vision and to improve overall.

Business Perspective

Organization-Level Performance Measurement

At the organization level, analysis should include profitability and overall shareholder value to make sure that CRM implementation is helping the company to achieve ROI. Performance analysis at this level will help the organization to establish the belief of achieving the CRM vision and sustaining it. Findings should be utilized to assess the overall organizational strategy. Performance data can guide the business strategy in terms of product and service offerings that will be required in order to satisfy current customer needs and to address future market trends.

Customer-Level Performance Measurement

At the customer level, performance indicators should include the perceived customer satisfaction and experience. Customer performance data should be analyzed to outline behavior patterns involving purchasing and complaining. In addition, customer loyalty and participation in reward schemes must be monitored because they also influence profit and growth in the long term. Measuring customer performance will only be worthwhile, however, if the changes in CRM strategy are being taken into consideration. Behavioral patterns contain hints for future customer needs and wants; therefore, appropriate actions toward satisfying those needs will be necessary.

Technology Perspective

At the process level, CRM strategy initiates several activities that aim to achieve different purposes that are mostly related to customers. More specifically, the goals are to acquire, satisfy, and retain customers. Keeping track of such activities is essential for achieving the desired performance at both the organization and customer levels. At the infrastructure level, performance analysis should indicate the positive influence of the CRM strategy within the IT and human relations units. Employees and technology play equal roles in CRM success, and, therefore, the CRM performance analysis should include them both. Conclusively, management should make sure that a monitoring and tracking mechanism exists to measure the CRM project's performance. The focus should be on continuous improvement, which is only possible if there is a feedback system in place and working. Finally, considering the fact that an organization may have to rely on intangible results while assessing CRM performance, the people involved in analysis should be unbiased and willing to go the extra mile.

Case 6. IBM Success Story

It is very important to be aware of the challenges faced in CRM implementation and to know how to overcome them. IBM's giant CRM project, which started in the year 2000, provides a learning example of implementing a CRM solution in a big, multinational company. This example highlights the state of affairs that led IBM management into considering a CRM solution, the process followed by the company to implement the CRM solution, the challenges faced by them during this process, and the benefits reaped by IBM after the implementation.

With new challenges and opportunities in the global marketplace, IBM was aiming to achieve superiority among its competitors in terms of sales, marketing, and customer service excellence. The company wanted to transform their business model to focus more on speed, efficiency, and responsiveness. After rounds of brainstorming sessions, the management concluded that to shape the customer experiences, while also generating added revenues and cost efficiencies, the first requirement would be to know their customers better. They decided to seek better collaboration with customers and among various IBM units involving sales, marketing, and support.

Keeping these goals at the forefront, IBM initiated a CRM project with full support from top management. In a broader sense, the company aimed to construct a unified interface linking the organization and its customers around the world. Specifically, the project was supposed to make certain that any interaction between the customer and the company, irrespective of any particular channel or country, took a uniform pattern and provided customers with a standardized level of service by using similar tools and information.

Considering the size and scope of the project, IBM decided to implement its CRM solution in multiple stages to make sure that each phase was concluded successfully before moving to the next one. The management knew that to serve customers well, the organization would need customer-oriented people, process, and technology. Separately, they had all three elements. IBM employees, especially salespeople, are well respected in the marketplace for helping customers transform their business with the help of different IBM products and services. Processes were already there, and technology was coming through the CRM solution. IBM recognized that it was the "integration" of all three elements that would pose a challenge. It was only through successful integration that the company would be able to redefine their internal customer service organization.

Handling several glitches along the way, the CRM deployment led to noteworthy improvement in several different units of IBM. Management reported that greater numbers of calls were dealt with and more leads were generated with the same number of employees working at a call center. Within a span of 4 years, the company reported that the level of customer satisfaction was up, fulfilling IBM's ultimate goal.

Source: IBM (n.d.).

CHAPTER 7

Achieving Full Integration for Maximum Performance

The integration of systems and processes should be a top priority for customer relationship management (CRM) system implementation. As members of any given business, employees, customers, and partners spend a lot of time searching for information. These efforts should be channeled toward gaining productivity and reducing service costs. For an organization, a standalone CRM system will not do any good until all of the applications are integrated and information is properly gathered, organized, and made accessible. For example, most of the organizations have established a link between front-end processes and back-office applications. Therefore, a CRM system, as a new entrant, should be capable of accommodating the already-established integration; otherwise, the firm will face disjointed databases and information silos.

Integration of external systems also poses a great challenge to CRM system implementation. Organized, simple, faster, and cheaper integration is every company's dream but one that is difficult to realize. Companies are finding that integration solutions designed from the bottom up, utilizing industry standard technology tools and processes, are better able to leverage integration choices. Especially in the case of hosted CRM solutions, integration with other systems is necessary in order to keep up a cohesive system of records. In any organization, it should be a top priority for the information technology (IT) division to maintain a unified data set, and their task should be considered part of an organization-wide strategy.

CRM Culture

The full integration of a CRM system into an organization's existing business architecture requires the establishment of CRM culture within the organization through company-wide awareness and implementation. Integration has to occur over a reasonable amount of time, and senior management needs to make sure that the CRM philosophy is completely developed and adopted. The CRM culture will place the customer in the center of each operational activity both inside and outside of the organization. Every employee must understand the customer in the context of CRM. Identifying and meeting customer needs should be seen as the basic purpose of work. Customer needs and wants should be integrated into organization's CRM program; more specifically, the evolution of the CRM culture should take place at several levels and on different dimensions, some of which are discussed in this chapter.

Employees

Considering the fact that initial trust building starts between customers and the firm's employees, a CRM program cannot be successful without customer-oriented employees who are willing to embrace the CRM culture. As the old saying goes, one cannot do a good job serving food to others with an empty stomach; hence, satisfied employees are a necessary resource for making customers happy. The bond between an organization and its customers breaks when an employee leaves the company; thus, making sure that employees are satisfied is also a critical part of a CRM culture-building process.

Businesses talk about customer retention as one of the key objectives of CRM programs but tend to forget that the retention of good employees is the first step in that direction. The longer the good employees stay with the organization, the more they become familiar with its operations, and employees who know the organization can really help the company achieve its CRM objectives.

Operations and Activities

Organization-wide CRM culture requires the matching of technology with a company's structure and priorities related to customers. Companies need to revise operational designs and evaluation metrics to monitor culture and CRM implementation so that business processes are aligned with CRM. The traditional philosophy is that a company's marketing operations division is the only one responsible for serving customers; this has to change since it is very counterproductive. Instead, the company should form cross-functional teams involving representatives from marketing, sales, research and development, production development, quality maintenance, and logistics. These teams should be assigned to gather technical and commercial information on customers and to reengineer the operational formats of the company. In addition, the organization should outline a development plan for integrating different operations and encouraging employees to become customer-centric.

Investment in new activities that are customer-focused is also an important consideration for organizations. The marketplace is evolving and so are customer needs. Serving the customer will require the organization to offer new and innovative products and services. Meeting the evolving needs of the customer will help the company to keep loyal customers. The marketing mix's (product, price, place, and promotion) activities will probably need readjustments in an organization with a dominant CRM culture. Marketing activities should attempt to convert "communication between a business and customer" into "interaction between two parties in a relationship."

Management

The development initiatives of a CRM culture will go nowhere without unwavering support from the management. CRM implementation will require a new attitude among executives, which will not be easy to achieve. Some senior-level executives who have operational expertise and strategic vision should oversee the CRM program's progress. Managers who, over time, have established credibility among peers and subordinates should be on the forefront and should set examples as early adopters of CRM cultural norms and values.

Mangers must adopt the new norms and values that have emerged through the development of a CRM culture, and employees at all levels in the organization will require a new reward and control system from the top management. Often, the control and reward system fails to recognize the value of effective customer service and ends up promoting efficiency of the processes so that more can be achieved in less time. This is not a long-term approach and does not align with CRM values. Both effective and efficient handling of operations is required to serve customers better and to retain them in the long run. Management may want to establish a separate central unit at the level of the vice president to keep the CRM activities intact.

The positive outcomes of CRM for the company are different from those of the customers. The outcomes of CRM enhance the company's ability to serve customers better. For employees, it is easy to determine the increases in revenue and the number of customers; however, management needs to do a better job conveying complex and inestimable benefits of CRM to employees. For example, management needs to emphasize the benefits of CRM adoption by explaining its contribution in establishing competitive differentiation that does not let the company's products become commodities.

Integration Into Value Chain

Delivering superior value to customers is the ultimate goal of adopting CRM culture; therefore, an organization should continuously invest in new business processes and marketing programs that enhance its value offerings. After each transaction, customers should feel that they are receiving greater value for the money they spent during that exchange. Today's customers are faced with complex purchasing decisions and buying processes that present organizations with opportunities to offer value at several points during the buying process. CRM should be integrated into the value chain so that customers can be provided with positive experiences when facing product performance or buying process related problems, shopping for affordable prices, and going through cognitive dissonance. With the help of CRM, an organization will be better able to build positive experience by answering questions effectively and efficiently, outlining competitive analysis, and informing customers about new and improved products. Therefore, integration of CRM into the value chain will require its presence in each marketing mix element: product, price, place, and promotion.

The company and the customer are both active participants in the value cocreation process. At the product level, CRM should be used to help new-product development teams profile, identify, and encourage customers to participate in this process. Use of CRM systems should increase the effectiveness of promotions by limiting redundancies and supporting customizations. In terms of distribution support, CRM systems should be used to integrate traditional marketing channels with new, online channels to create a "bricks and clicks" approach so that customers are able to access and purchase products through physical retail locations as well as through company website or other online venues. Finally, price determination should be conducted alongside CRM implementation. Some customers are looking for a premium service that comes with a premium price, such as a passenger who bought a business-class airplane ticket. On the other hand, some customers want price breaks in order to be satisfied. CRM should be a part of such price determination activities in order to generate a loyal customer base.

Integration Across Channels

Customers touch the various components of an organization, and the outcomes of these contacts shape their perceptions of the organization, its services, and its products. A CRM program should encompass the entire organization and improve the integration of cross-functional initiatives. A fragmented business architecture often undermines the performance. To serve customers well, departments and channels need to be integrated. For example, the corporate team may come up with the best marketing communication strategy; however, until this strategy is aligned with the tactics performed by company's communication channels, it is impossible to achieve the desired objectives. To realize the full potential of CRM, all channels within an organization need to be integrated. Moreover, CRM itself provides a good interface for connecting different channels for different purposes. CRM software and customer databases may help individual channels or departments to improve their own specific activities while maintaining a comprehensive customer-centric approach at the organizational level.

The growth of CRM systems among businesses has accelerated the advancement of techniques and applications that go along with CRM applications. Technological innovations that can help organizations integrate their operation are especially getting a lot of attention. For example, Web Service, a new technique that has emerged, is well on its way to becoming the synonym for business applications integration. Web Service uses XML and Simple Object Access Protocol (SOAP) to transport data over the Internet and allows multiple applications to interact with each other without complex custom coding. Web services are different from web applications as they generally involve application-to-application interaction and are not accessed through a web browser. Interestingly, a web-services integration approach can be extended to third-party organizations such as business partners, dealers, or customers. This technique allows companies to interact with each other behind a firewall so that they do not have to worry about the revelation of personal knowledge regarding each other's IT systems. This empowers firms to integrate both inside and outside of the organization.

Another big problem associated with the lack of channel integration is inconsistent information sharing between channels within the company. Often, sales and customer service employees have little visibility of the web channel, and websites sometimes have weak correlations with other information sources. This lack of integration supports the development of "information silos" within an organization, which is very unproductive and lethal for the customer relationship-building process. Without an integrated approach, a customer has to deal with multiple departments that may not convey the same information (see Figure 7.1). This mismatching of information degrades the customer experience. On the other hand, if communication channels are interconnected and information is accessed through a CRM system, customers receive constructive information sharing with organization.

Communication facilitates the relationship-building process by resolving disputes, aligning objectives, and revealing new opportunities for involved parties. Since the customer is a participant in the value creation process, and the customer should therefore be treated as an internal entity residing within the organizational loop, the communication of

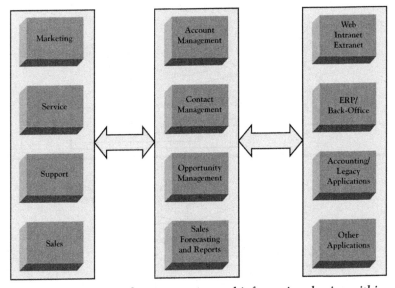

Figure 7.1. *Customer-firm interaction and information sharing within the firm.*

information between marketing channels and customers should be considered a top priority.

The CRM system will improve the flow of precise information across channels and the company's overall goal of building stronger relationships with their customers (see Figure 7.2). For example, during the exchange process, with the help of CRM tools, salespeople can modify large amounts of data into a more functional form that can be transferred to customers in an organized manner. Additionally, CRM use will facilitate salespeople's evaluation of alternative proposals and help them present data in graphical and tabular formats to better communicate a recommendation.

Data Analytics for Identifying Customer Lifetime Value

The current economic environment has forced senior management to demand higher levels of marketing effectiveness and higher profits while offering the same, or an even lower, marketing budget. Top management often ignores emerging challenges faced by marketing units. For example, the business marketplace is witnessing a vast amount of

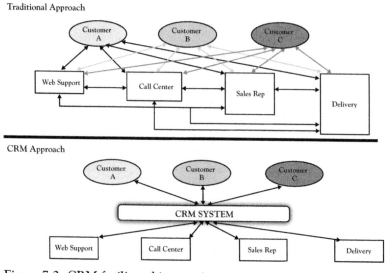

Figure 7.2. CRM *facilitated integration.*

market fragmentation and extensive channel proliferation, leading to increased customer expectations and demands. To tackle this situation, marketers are relying on customer analytics in order to have sound customer knowledge and better control over marketing outcomes.

Oftentimes, organizations struggle to find out why they are not making enough money to recover from their initial expenditures on capital. One reason why they may not find the underlying cause is that they may not have considered their unprofitable customers. Doing business with this type of customer reduces the firm's profits and negatively affects shareholder value. Realizing the full potential of a customer relationship and calculating the true customer value are complex puzzles and pose serious challenges to any organization. The organization's goal is to have a relationship with a customer that ultimately leads to profits. CRM can help businesses realize their goal of making every customer as valuable as possible over the lifetime of the relationship.

A business should know the key drivers of customer lifetime value (CLV). As mentioned earlier, CLV can be defined as the present value of the future cash flows attributed to a specific customer relationship. Use of CLV as a marketing metric tends to place greater emphasis on customer service and long-term customer satisfaction than on maximizing short-term sales. Some of these drivers are targeting costs, acquisition costs, service costs, usage revenue, service revenue, and relationship duration. Customer value modeling, on the other hand, involves the firm's assessment of other customer features, such as the ability to introduce other profitable customers to the organization, the possibility of becoming a more profitable customer in the future, and so on. Any of these objectives are possible to achieve if the company has very rich customer data. Businesses have repeatedly complained that access to relevant data and the quality of already collected data are some of the toughest challenges to overcome.

Advances in technology have made it possible to collect customer information through various customer touch points and other sources. Technology offers solutions that may lead a business toward a more comprehensive understanding of the needs of their customers by employing customer knowledge repositories and data analytics. Yet, it is important to recognize that not all this happened overnight, and it is essential to understand the growth of the technology and techniques. Understanding the growth of the technology and techniques related to CRM is also important because it demonstrates the growing importance of data analytics.

Evolution of Data Analysis Technology

Data analysis, as a critical business practice, has come a long way since its early inception. With the launch of computers and disks in the 1960s, businesses saw the potential of data analysis. Yet, most of the analysis was retrospective and static in nature. For example, finding out average sales over the last 3 years is retrospective. Development in the field of programming facilitated the emergence of relational databases in the 1980s. Characteristics of such technology involved retrospective but dynamic data access.

Next came the era of multidimensional databases, thus allowing businesses to perform data navigation. Online analytical processing (OLAP) and data warehousing became essential technologies for businesses to have. OLAP is one great technology that provided the basis for effective and efficient executive information systems (EIS) solutions. As a result of integrating OLAP and data warehousing techniques, businesses could amass huge amounts of data in a very easy and presentable format. With EIS calculations, managers can address interesting but complex questions. OLAP and EIS solutions also enable executives to interactively browse through their firm's multilayer business processes.

Executives and decision makers want to look beyond static report contents to discover the key variables that inflict or influence operational results. OLAP analysis is one good method for realizing this goal because it provides users with a greater degree of report flexibility, presentation, and performance analysis. OLAP reporting enables users to alter reporting structures and redevelop views by just "dragging and dropping" multiple dimensions on top of the analysis presentation. With OLAP applications, the reports are not limited to predefined segments and filters; instead, reports are fairly dynamic in terms of overall format and structure. In addition, processing time for reports does not slow down even when there is a large amount of data.

Currently, businesses are at the data mining stage, where huge databases and strong multiprocessors make prospective and proactive information delivery possible. Data mining uses advanced parallel algorithms, applied statistics, and high-performance computers to discover the knowledge from databases. Some other innovations, such as metadata, helped control the quality of entering data into the database.

Knowledge Discovery Through Data Mining

Companies are motivated to explore databases and discover information like never before. The business environment is changing with demanding customers and thinner market segments. Thus, organizations are collecting more and more data, causing databases to grow at an unprecedented rate. On the other hand, pressure is mounting to make decisions quickly but deliberately. All of this has fueled technology innovations and business practices to concentrate on data mining. Data mining involves the exploration, analysis, and visualization of data from a huge database without having a particular hypothesis to test. Through advanced data search abilities and statistical algorithms, patterns and correlations are extracted from the data set. Data mining helps businesses discover novel, implicit, and useful information that cannot be extracted through manual efforts.

New and advanced sales analytics applications have enabled sales managers to perform complex data mining in CRM and sales force automation systems. With more data being fed into CRM systems and advanced analytics being used, sales managers are able to do their jobs more effectively. For example, managers are able to see deals that are lost and analyze why, identify salespeople who need additional coaching on particular issues, and filter out nonproductive selling approaches. Add-on systems that can be integrated with a company's existing CRM and business applications are also available in the market. Core CRM solution providers have also enhanced the analytics capabilities of their systems. Overall, sales managers and sales representatives are in a better situation to make informed decisions and maximize their performance.

Sales and marketing operations benefit the most from data mining applications. In almost all business settings, data mining can help businesses outline discrete market segments beyond traditional analysis by considering additional variables. Some of the critical applications include the following:

- *Basket analysis* determines what items customers usually purchase as a bundle. Inventory management, retail store layout strategies, and sales promotions can benefit tremendously from this information.
- *Sales forecasting* is analyzing customers' time-based patterns, such as if a customer buys a product this week, when is the next purchase most likely to happen.
- *Database marketing* is developing and managing marketing communications based on customer data. This may enable businesses to develop customer profiles to launch cost-effective marketing campaigns. For example, knowing the certain behaviors of customers, such as who always picks premium brands, can help a retailer customize its promotions.

Case 7. CRM System at Toyota France: An Integrated Approach

The world's largest carmaker, Toyota, operates in France through a distribution network composed of 200 partners and 300 resellers. Having such a wide operational scope, the company's French management felt the need for a comprehensive information system that help them restructure, modernize, and simplify the sales process and direct marketing activities.

Seeking to select an appropriate system, Toyota France conducted a survey with a focus on customer relationship management optimization throughout its distribution network. Management wanted to equip all resellers and partners of the company with one solution that would manage sales and marketing processes in a centralized and integrated fashion. One of the primary goals was to come up with one sales activity center that could manage the complete customer relationship chain. To make it work, the management wanted the new center to be properly interfaced with existing systems and easy to use. In a broader sense, this central unit was supposed to provide resellers and executive management with high performing analytical functionalities.

The management was well aware of the complexity of the task and therefore decided to select the long-term partner AXOA to conduct the survey, implement the solution, and organize information collected from the resellers and partners. AXOA, a rapidly emerging company in the CRM market, carries a mission to accompany and streamline the CRM-related needs of its clients. After successfully completing the research study in early 2008, AXOA made its recommendations. Toyota France selected Pivotal CRM from CDC Software. This CRM system has been implemented in approximately 300 reseller locations, and information from a centralized unit is being shared by more than 1,000 users.

With the help of dedicated users, the combined project team of Toyota France, AXOA, and Pivotal CRM integrated and deployed the project smoothly. The CRM system is customized with the company's needs, specifically, management of sales cycles, measurement of traffic, analysis of sales, and influence of marketing communication activities. The current CRM solution has enabled Toyota France to integrate processes from car sales to product coding and to facilitate operations in sales, marketing, and customer services. Front-end employees are better able to answer the broad CRM needs of customers, thus helping them to do business in their respective markets.

Source: Business Wire (2009, June 9).

CHAPTER 8

Technology Assessment, Maintenance, and Adaptation

For an organization to get the most out of a customer relationship management (CRM) technology investment, it is essential to appraise current technology use in different processes and provide a baseline for how CRM technology is being used. Such appraisal should involve interviewing employees and managers in order to understand the objectives for the organization and recommending areas where technology could positively affect those objectives. The widely used technique to achieve this goal is the technology audit.

Technique

As a method of assessment, a technology audit aims to investigate technology capability, processes, and requirements of a concerned firm. Through this evaluation exercise, an organization is able to identify the strengths and weaknesses of its overall technology infrastructure. The technology audit leads to concrete proposals through a process of analysis including information collection and synthesis. In other words, after completion, it will result in an action plan leading to technological improvement and acquisition of needed technologies and expertise.

Although similar techniques exist, they differ from the technology audit in one way or another. For example, some organizations do not want to hire an external party; instead, they opt for an internal assessment, which is usually referred to as a self-evaluation audit. Another procedure is benchmarking, where analysis is done through comparison with the leader in the market or average of all the companies within the relevant industrial sector.

Objectives

The common goals of a technology audit are to assess organizations regarding their capabilities of incorporating the latest technologies and their ability to work and align with their technological partners. As a result, the technology audit outlines what firms need to do to successfully incorporate a supportive and productive technology infrastructure. For example, a technology audit will exemplify the needs of a firm related to sales growth from different strategic points, such as revising the product management strategy that can sharpen the competitive edge and technological areas that need attention to successfully execute this strategy, or finding ways for technology transfer, training, and development to fuel sustainable growth.

Benefits

For firms that decide to go through this exercise, the benefits are numerous. In today's highly competitive and technology-enabled business environment, it is essential to keep a vigilant eye on one of the key resources of an organization: its technology. A technology audit can result in a detailed analysis and evaluation of the technology needs of the concerned firm, which are critical for achieving and maintaining sustainable growth. A comprehensive and professional situation analysis (strength, weakness, opportunity, and threat), or SWOT, by an external, unbiased party can provide the firm with a prescription for remedying internal and external problems. It will help a firm to not only spot opportunities for new technologies and services but also get connected with other technology suppliers and sources that can assist the firm in exploring such opportunities completely.

Structure

External experts in association with internal staff carry out the technology audit. There are no standard guidelines for performing a technology audit, yet it is often composed of some typical steps such as initial preparation, general diagnosis, information collection, summarization, report presentation, and implementation follow-up. Specifically, the first step, preparation, involves the broad understanding of the industry in which the firm operates as well as the firm's current position and status of its network with other firms and technology partners. A general diagnosis requires the collection and analysis of general information and a brief presentation to receive early feedback and reaction on direction and approach that leads to a detailed data collection campaign. The information collection process includes detailed interviews with top management and administrators regarding their strategy and investment plans; with the operations and productions fleet regarding productivity, technology adaptability, and safety and maintenance issues; with the research and development (R&D) people regarding the status and type of R&D activities; with the human resource managers regarding training, current capabilities, and available resources; and with the sales and marketing team regarding marketing strategy and tactics, competitors, and sales force automation.

The technology audit team then prepares a detailed report summarizing the outcome of analysis and synthesis of information. This report creates the groundwork for an action plan that aims to address any technological problems and issues surfacing from the audit. Next, the presentation component includes an open discussion with the management and executives regarding the recommendations and findings and delineation of the action plan. Finally, the last step of a technology audit involves follow-up visits to help, support, and provide direction to the management regarding the implementation of the action plan.

Relevance

A technology audit is extremely relevant to firms with top management that is serious about future strategy and motivated to improve from within the firm. This seriousness involves willingness and financial commitment to the technology audit. The firms that are committed to developing new products, incorporating novel technology, enhancing potential, and integrating their work processes are ideal candidates for technology audits. Apart from motivation to conduct an audit, management needs to make sure that it is feasible to invest in this process, considering resources, employees, turnover, and sufficient internal capabilities for implementing a novel idea or carrying out an innovative project. This technique is uniformly appropriate to both service and manufacturing organizations that consist of 15 to 350 employees.

Auditors

An external party, an individual auditor, or a team of auditors performs a technology audit. Technology auditors can be classified as either generalists or specialists. Generalists are experienced and qualified consultants in the industry. Professionally, they are capable of performing analysis and carry great knowledge of the relevant business environment, such as market trends, needs, and technology infrastructure. On a personal front, they are active listeners and positive thinkers. They have great endurance and follow a practical approach.

Specialists, on the other hand, have expertise and experience in a specific sector or technology. They are recognizable and well-known experts in the field yet possess a global perspective. Such auditors can be extremely helpful if an organization has narrowed down a problem area and is looking for expedited problem identification and solution.

Implementation

Actual implementation of a technology audit technique provides an organization with a complete view of their technology infrastructure. Implementation requires commitment from both the organization and technology auditor chosen for the job. Among top management, there should be strong and complete consensus for going through the technology audit so that people within the organization are open and collaborative with the auditor. More importantly, management and executives should be motivated and determined to execute the action plan emerged through this exercise; otherwise, the time and investment will go in vain. On the other side, the auditor(s) should make sure the trust mechanism with the management is in place and working. Different auditors may do things as per their own style; however, the basic steps of a technology audit should be followed. The 10 basic steps of any technology audit include the following:

1. The process starts with the organization's decision to carry out the technology audit. The motivation for this can come from both internal and external sources. Some of the trigger points of the management's desire to perform a technology audit are stagnant sales growth, disintegration among departments, rejuvenation of the organizational structure, and competitors' adaptability of new technology. In some cases, firms are approached by external consultants or experts explaining the scope of such initiatives and citing the benefits of this technique. Irrespective of the cause that fuels the company's desire, as a first step, company needs to *firmly* decide that they are willing to do it and that they are capable of doing it.

2. If the decision to implement the technology audit comes from internal sources, then the second step would be to pick an auditor (see previous section for a detailed discussion). Management should keep in mind that they are not looking for a celebrity to endorse their firm; instead, they are in search of a professional who has expertise relevant to the firm.

3. After deciding on the auditor, the preparation for the technology audit speeds up and the auditor takes the driver's seat. During initial visits, the auditor outlines the steps to follow and, if possible, conducts a formal presentation regarding the process of technology audit to make sure the management and key executives are on the same page.

4. At this step, the auditor starts collecting data in order to get a clearer view of the firm's internal and external environments. Data about the firm mostly come from published information, websites, brochures, annual reports, and so on. The auditor would also be interested in knowing about the industry, the trends, the market, and the technology introduction, adoption, and use.

5. Narrowing the domain, the auditor starts focusing on specific details and performs a basic diagnosis by researching the human resources, existing technological capacity and future needs, innovation capabilities, product and service offerings, quality management, and marketing and sales operations.

6. Based on data analysis, the auditor then creates a report containing snapshots of the firm's activities, an overview of market, and the results of the preliminary SWOT analysis. The primary purpose

of this diagnostic report is to outline existing problems and their potential solutions, strengths, and opportunities.

7. The next step is to present the first diagnosis report to the top management and other responsible groups. The objective is to highlight routes for solutions with an action plan. If necessary, the auditor may put forward the proposal that rationalizes their decision to further analyze a particular business unit, if doing so can help distinguish the problem area. A detailed rationale will be essential for making sure that the particular unit does not feel isolated.

8. Depending on the specific department that needs further diagnosis, the auditing team may have particular objectives for that department's analysis. For example, the human relations unit will require analysis of the reward-promotion system, teamwork culture, project management, and employee training. Operation units will require the diagnosis of its system automation, material flow process, productivity, and so on. The marketing and sales departments will be analyzed in terms of their market plan, e-commerce and Internet operations, sales force automation, opportunities and threats, and so on.

9. At this point, the auditor concludes the final version of the audit report and presents it to the top management and other concerned groups. The audit report is expected to provide the firm with a summary of results from diagnostics, analysis of data, methodology used for analysis, identified problems, suggested solutions, and a detailed action plan.

10. The final step of a technology audit resembles the *servicing the sale* approach that involves follow-up visits to help, support, and provide direction to the management regarding the implementation of the action plan.

Notes

Chapter 1

1. Metcalfe (1995), p. 4.
2. Dickie (2008, May).
3. Dickie (2008, December).

Chapter 2

1. Newman (2009, October), p. 20.

Chapter 4

1. Dyché (2002).
2. Schein (1990).

Chapter 6

1. Kim and Kim (2008).

References

On the Web

Baker, P. (2008, April 24). The 10 most useless CRM-system features. Retrieved from http://www.insidecrm.com/features/10-useless-crm-features-042408/

Bass, A. (2003). Cigna's self-inflicted wounds: A cautionary tale about the peril of IT transformation and the dangers of counting your chickens before they hatch. Retrieved from http://www.cio.com.au/article/181174/cigna_self-inflicted_wounds?pp=1

Binary Spectrum. (2010, May 23). Key functionalities of CRM software. Retrieved from http://www.binaryspectrum.com/industries/retail/Key -Functionalities-of-CRM.html

Bucholtz, C. (2009, June 15). Is there a service innovation shortage? Retrieved from http://www.insidecrm.com/blog/is-there-a-service-innovation-shortage.php

Business Wire. (2009, June 9). Toyota France uses pivotal CRM for managing sales activity of its reseller network. Retrieved from http://www.businesswire.com

Campbell, S. J. (2007, March 30). Key points to remember after purchasing CRM software. Retrieved from http://www.tmcnet.com

CDC Software. (2009, June). Toyota France uses pivotal CRM for managing sales activity of its reseller network. Retrieved from http://www.cdcsoftware.com/en/Company/News-and-Events/Press-Releases.aspx

Channel Pro. (2009, April 2). While ERP sales are set to fall in 2009, spending on CRM software will increase, says IDC. Retrieved from http://www.channelpro.co.uk/news/228736/erp_to_take_a_hit_in_2009_but_crm _looking_strong.html

Cook, R. (2009, April 7). Five principles of CRM security: Protect yourself from data theft and misuse with this five-point guide to CRM security. Retrieved from http://www.insidecrm.com/features/checklist-crm-security-040709

Craig, R. (1999, February 17). The evolution of CRM applications–customer relationship management–industry trend or event. Retrieved from http://findarticles.com/p/articles/mi_m0FOX/is_4_4/i_54299254/?tag=content;col1

Dickie, J. (2008, December). Assessing the state of the CRM space. *Software Magazine.* Retrieved from http://www.softwaremag.com/L.cfm?Doc =1189-12/2008

Dickie, J. (2008, May). The ever-expanding CRM platform. *Software Magazine.* Retrieved from http://www.softwaremag.com/L.cfm?Doc=1125-4/2008

Duffy, C. (2006, August 28). How to calculate CRM total cost of ownership. Retrieved from http://www.webpronews.com/expertarticles/2006/08/28/how-to-calculate-crm-total-cost-of-ownership

Dyché, J. (2002, February 1). Scoping and prioritizing CRM projects. Retrieved from http://www.informit.com/articles/article.aspx?p=25181&seqNum=4

Edwards, J. (2007, September 13). Your data secure with hosted CRM? Security considerations when using an external service provider and sizing up the enemy within. Retrieved from http://www.insidecrm.com/features/hosted-crm-data-safety-091307

Fleischer, J. (2002, December 01). The scope of CRM: How much customer relationship management can companies really afford? Retrieved from http://www.callcentermagazine.com/showArticle.jhtml?articleID=8702058

Hosted CRM vs. in-house: Which direction should your company take? (2009). Retrieved from http://www.insidecrm.com/whitepaper/pdf/hosted%20vs%20inhouse.pdf

IBM. (n.d.). IBM takes customer service to the next level. Retrieved from http://www-07.ibm.com/services/pdf/alliances_siebel_story.pdf

ICFAI Center for Management Research. (2002). CRM/KM initiatives at 3M: A case study. Retrieved from http://www.icmrindia.org/casestudies/catalogue/IT%20and%20Systems/ITSY010.htm

Kane, R. (2004). The top 10 myths of hosted CRM. *ASPadvocate.* Retrieved from http://www.crmlandmark.com/library/10MythsofHostedCRMWhitepaper.pdf

Maclaren, P. J., & Frankel, E. (2002). Building an effective web-based CRM infrastructure. Retrieved from http://www.akenbros.com/archive/MGMT345/Lectures/ch08.doc

Marketing Find. (2005). Where are small and medium-sized e-businesses going with CRM. Retrieved from http://www.marketingfind.com/articles/where_are_small_and_mediumsized_ebusinesses_going_with_crm.html

Mesure, S. (2003, October 10). Loyalty card costs Tesco £1bn of profits - but is worth every penny. Retrieved from http://www.independent.co.uk/news/business/analysis-and-features/loyalty-card-costs-tesco-acircpound1bn-of-profits--but-is-worth-every-penny-582877.html

Microsoft Dynamics. (2005). Leading asset manager creates single global customer view for improved account management. Customer solution case study. Retrieved from http://www.microsoft.com/industry/financialservices/banking/solutions/customer_knowledge/default.mspx

Newman, R. (2009, October 5). 10 Retailers Gaining Strength From the Recession. *US News and World Report.* Retrieved from http://www.usnews.com/

money/blogs/flowchart/2009/10/05/10-retailers-gaining-strength-from-the -recession.html

Pombriant, D. (2005). Aplicor helps Host.net build processes. A case study by Beagle Research Group. Retrieved from http://www.aplicoronline.eu/pdf/ BeagleResearchCaseStudy.pdf

Sage CRM. (2005). How to choose a hosted CRM system. Sage Software. Retrieved from http://www.marshallpoe.com/solutions/SageCRM/How ToChooseHostedCRM.pdf

SearchSMBAsia Editors. (2009, May 22). ASEAN SMBs to increase spending on CRM software. Retrieved from http://www.searchsmbasia.com/en/content/ asean-smbs-increase-spending-crm-software

Watson, Brian P. (2007, March 8). 5 tips for deploying on-demand CRM. Retrieved from http://www.baselinemag.com/c/a/Projects-Customer -Service/5-Tips-for-Deploying-OnDemand-CRM/

Weinberger, J. (2004, August 13). IDC predicts $11.4 billion in CRM application sales in 2008. Retrieved from http://www.destinationcrm.com/Articles/ CRM-News/Daily-News/IDC-Predicts-$11.4-Billion-in-CRM-Application -Sales-in-2008-47256.aspx

Wells Fargo invests in customers with PeopleSoft Enterprise CRM. (2001). Retrieved from http://www.crmadvocate.com/casestudy/peoplesoft/ wellsfargo_45.pdf

Publications and Documents

Ahearne, M., Jelinek, R., & Rapp, A. (2005). Moving beyond the direct effect of SFA adoption on salesperson performance: Training and support as key moderating factors. *Industrial Marketing Management, 34*, 379–388.

Ahearne, M., Jones, E., Rapp, A., & Mathieu, J. (2008). High touch through high tech: The impact of salesperson technology usage on sales performance via mediating mechanisms. *Management Science, 54*(4), 671–685.

Ahearne, M., Srinivasan, N., & Weinstein, L. (2004). Effect of technology on sales performance: Progressing from technology acceptance to technology usage and consequence. *Journal of Personal Selling & Sales Management, 24*(4), 297–310.

Anderson, R. E., & Dubinsky, A. J. (2004). *Personal selling: Achieving customer satisfaction and loyalty*. Boston, MA: Houghton Mifflin.

Avlonitis, G. J., & Panagopoulos, N. G. (2005). Antecedents and consequences of CRM technology acceptance in the sales force. *Industrial Marketing Management, 34*(4), 355–368.

Buttle, F. A. (2006). Hosted CRM: Literature review and research questions. MGSM Working Papers in Management, Macquarie Graduate School of Management, MGSM WP 2006-1.

Colombo, G. W. (1994). *Sales force automation.* New York, NY: McGraw-Hill.

Cotteleer, M., Inderrieden, E., & Lee, F. (2006). Selling the sales force on automation. *Harvard Business Review, 84*(10), 144.

Dyché, J. (2001). *The CRM handbook: A business guide to customer relationship management.* Toronto, Canada: Addison-Wesley Professional.

Engle, R. L., & Barnes, M. L. (2000). Sales force automation usage, effectiveness, and cost-benefit in Germany, England and the United States. *Journal of Business and Industrial Marketing, 15*(4), 216–241.

Erffmeyer, R. C., & Johnson, D. A. (2001). An exploratory study of sales force automation practices: Expectations and realities. *Journal of Personal Selling & Sales Management, 21*(2), 167–175.

Geiger, S., & Turley, D. (2006). The perceived impact of information technology on salespeople's relational competencies. *Journal of Marketing Management, 22*, 827–851.

Hart, S., Hogg, G., & Banerjee, M. (2004). Does the level of experience have an effect on CRM programs? Exploratory research findings. *Industrial Marketing Management, 33*, 549–560.

Honeycutt, E. D., Jr., Thelen, T., Thelen, S. T., & Hodge, S. K. (2005). Impediments to sales force automation. *Industrial Marketing Management, 34*, 313–322.

Huber, G. P. (1991, February). Organizational learning: The contributing processes and the literatures. *Organization Science, 2*, 88–115.

Humby, C., Hunt, T., & Phillips, T. (2004). Scoring points: How Tesco is winning customer loyalty, London, UK: Kogan Page.

Hunter, G. K., & Perreault, W. D., Jr. (2007, January). Making sales technology effective. *Journal of Marketing, 71*, 16–34.

InnoSupport. (2005). Supporting innovation in SMEs. *Leonardo da Vinci Pilot Project Report*, 10–15.

Jain, S. C. (2005). CRM shifts the paradigm. *Journal of Strategic Marketing, 13*, 275–291.

Jones, E., Sundaram, S., & Chin, W. (2002). Factors leading to sales force automation use: A longitudinal analysis. *Journal of Personal Selling & Sales Management, 22*(3), 145–156.

Kim, H.-S., & Kim, Y.-G. (2008). A CRM performance measurement framework: Its development process and application. *Industrial Marketing Management, 38*(4), 477–489.

Ko, D.-G., & Dennism A. R. (2004). Sales force automation and sales performance: Do experience and expertise matter? *Journal of Personal Selling & Sales Management, 24*(4), 311–322.

Kotler, P. (1984). *Marketing essentials*, Englewood Cliffs, NJ: Prentice Hall.

Leigh, T. W., & Tanner, J. F., Jr. (2004). Introduction: JPSSM special issue on customer relationship management. *Journal of Personal Selling & Sales Management, 24*(4), 259–262.

Leonard-Barton, D., & Deschamps, I. (1988). Managerial influence in the implementation of new technology. *Managerial Science, 34*, 1252–1265.

Metcalfe, J. S. (1995). Technology systems and technology policy in an evolutionary framework. *Cambridge Journal of Economics, 19*, 25–46.

Morgan, A. J., & Inks, S. A. (2001). Technology and the sales force: Increasing acceptance of sales force automation. *Industrial Marketing Management, 30*, 463–472.

Orlikowski, W. J. (1992). The duality of technology: Rethinking the concept of technology in organizations. *Organization Science, 3*(3), 398–427.

Parathasarathy, M., & Sohi, R. S. (1997). Sales force automation and the adoption of technological innovations by salespeople: Theory and implications. *Journal of Business & Industrial Marketing, 12*(3/4), 196–208.

Pullig, C., Maxham, J. G., III, & Hair, J. F., Jr. (2002). Sales force automation systems: An exploratory examination of organizational factors associated with effective implementation and salesforce productivity. *Journal of Business Research, 55*, 401–415.

Rapp, A., Agnihotri, R., & Forbes, L. (2008). The sales force technology-performance chain: The role of adaptive selling and effort. *Journal of Personal Selling and Sales Management, 28*(4), 335–350.

Reichheld, F. F., & Sasser, W. E., Jr. (1990). Zero defections: Quality comes to services. *Harvard Business Review, 68*(5), 105–111.

Rigby, D. K., & Ledingham, D. (2004). CRM done right. *Harvard Business Review, 82*(11), 118–129.

Rigby, D. K., Reichheld, F. F., & Schefter, P. (2002). Avoid the four common perils of CRM. *Harvard Business Review, 80*(2), 101–109.

Rivers, M. L., & Dart, J. (1999). The acquisition and use of sales force automation by mid-sized manufacturers. *Journal of Personal Selling & Sales Management, 19*, 59–73.

Schein, E. (1985). *Organizational culture and leadership*. San Francisco, CA: Jossey-Bass.

Schein, E. (1990). Organizational culture. *American Psychologist, 45*, 109–119.

Schillewaert, N., Ahearne, M. J., Frambach, R. T., & Moenaert, R. K. (2005). The adoption of information technology in the sales force. *Industrial Marketing Management, 34*, 323–336.

Speier, C., & Venkatesh, V. (2002). The hidden minefields in the adoption of sales force automation technologies. *Journal of Marketing, 66*(3), 98–111.

Sundaram, S., Schwarz, A., Jones, E., & Chin, W. W. (2007). Technology use on the front line: How information technology enhances individual performance. *Journal of Academy of Marketing Science, 35,* 101–112.

Venkatesh, V., & Davis, F. D. (2000). A theoretical extension of the technology acceptance model: Four longitudinal field studies. *Management Science, 46*(2), 186–204.

Widmier, S. M., Jackson, D. W., Jr., & McCabe, D. B. (2002). Infusing technology into personal selling. *Journal of Personal Selling and Sales Management, 22*(3), 189–198.

Yin, F. H., Anderson, R. E., & Swaminathan, S. (2004). Customer relationship management: Its dimensions and effects on customer outcomes. *Journal of Personal Selling & Sales Management, 24*(4), 263–278.

Zikmund, W. G., McLeod, R., & Gilbert, F. W. (2003). *Customer relationship management.* Hoboken, NJ: Wiley.

Index

Note: The *f* following page numbers refers to figures.

CPSIA information can be obtained at www.ICGtesting.com
Printed in the USA
BVOW09s1819040515

398700BV00003B/80/P

9 781606 491270